OUR BAPTIST TRADITION

Smyth & Helwys Publishing, Inc.
6316 Peake Road
Macon, Georgia 31210-3960
1-800-747-3016
©2005 by Smyth & Helwys Publishing
All rights reserved.
Printed in the United States of America.

The paper used in this publication meets the minimum requirements of
American National Standard for Information Sciences—
Permanence of Paper for Printed Library Materials.
ANSI Z39.48–1984. (alk. paper)

Library of Congress Cataloging-in-Publication Data

Tuck, William Powell, 1934-
Our Baptist tradition / by William Powell Tuck.— Rev. ed.
p. cm.
Includes bibliographical references.
ISBN 1-57312-456-7 (pbk. : alk. paper)
1. Baptists.
I. Title.
BX6331.3.T83 2005
286—dc22

2005006132

OUR BAPTIST TRADITION

William Powell Tuck

Foreword

On and off over the years, I have taught a class titled "Religious Groups in America." In that class I focus on the Christian tradition and the differences between Christian groups in this country. Student interest in the subject has never waned; they are always eager to know why and where Christians differ. I hear it said today from many sources that "denominations as we have known them are dead in America." To be honest, I am not quite sure what people mean by such statements. Even if I understood, however, I would not agree. Thankfully, the petulant and bitter denominational rivalries—those between Baptists and Methodists, for example—are virtually dead. The real tension today in American religion is *intra*denominational rather than inter-denominational.

The need in American religion is not to turn away from our various denominational traditions. Rather it is to understand those traditions, their historical contexts, their theological claims, and their biblical preferences. Denominational traditions, like the biblical tradition, must be constantly reinterpreted and applied to new situations and needs. Understanding heritage, whether biblical, theological, or denominational, is an ongoing enterprise.

This is why Bill Tuck's book is important. It is a successful attempt to restate the Baptist tradition without misshaping it essence. It is important, in my judgment, that this statement comes from a Baptist pastor, one who understands how the heritage of Baptists connects with the needs of people in the pew.

Grady Nutt, a Christian funny man who died far too soon, spent much of his life trying to persuade college students to learn to love newer and bigger things without having to put the knock on their past. He illustrated by noting the disciples of John the Baptist who left John for Jesus. Grady said, "You've got to learn to love Jesus without knocking John." What you will find in these pages is not a provincial partisanship but a warm appreciation and commitment to the greater church of Jesus Christ. You will also find, however, a Baptist pastor-scholar speaking appreciatively and gratefully of his personal and denominational heritage. Tuck, unlike some, has learned to love the bigger church without forgetting the one where he first met the Holy in life. A careful study of these chapters will help a Baptist not only become a better Baptist, but a better Christian. For all their warts, that has been the intention of every Christian denomination ever born—to help produce better Christians.

Walter B. Shurden
Executive Director
The Center for Baptist Studies
Mercer University
Macon, Georgia

Preface

Baptists have a rich and wonderful heritage, but I have discovered through listening and reading that many people in Baptist churches are unfamiliar with this legacy. There are many fine books about Baptist history, but I have observed that few people, especially laypeople, are willing to read these lengthy books. In the chapters that follow, I have attempted to present our Baptist heritage in a few pages. I have been gratified at the interest and response to this study in churches I have served. This small book is an attempt to let others learn more about our beliefs.

The Baptist historian Robert G. Torbet has observed:

> The facts of history indicate that there has been some historical continuity prior to the Protestant Reformation of those basic principles which have characterized the people called Baptists, whose origin as a formal organizational entity may be traced with certainty from the seventeenth century and whose spiritual forebears constituted the radical wing of the Protestant Movement of the sixteenth century. That this heritage has not been forsaken by modern Baptists may be attested by a study of their history in the past three and a half centuries.[1]

Our recent history, however, makes us wonder if Baptists are not in danger of losing their distinctives. The response of my congregation has encouraged me to believe that many want to hold on to the beliefs that have characterized us since the seventeenth century. This small book is one effort to help our people carry forward the Baptist heritage into the next century.

I want to express my appreciation to Carolyn Stice, my former secretary, who typed these chapters through several drafts, and to Ida Helm and Ann Prentice, who served as proofreaders. I also want to thank congregations where I have served as pastor. Their encouragement has continued to motivate me in my study of our Baptist beliefs and practices. My prayer is that we will know, practice, teach, and cherish our Baptist heritage.

William Powell Tuck

NOTE

[1] Robert G. Torbet, *A History of the Baptists* (Philadelphia: Judson Press, 1950), 34.

CHAPTER ONE

Personal Religious Experience

If I stood before an average Baptist congregation and asked, "What do we believe as Baptists?" I expect I would be disappointed in some of the answers. People can usually state why they are members of a particular church, but their reason for being a Baptist often ends in generalizations. Many do not have much awareness of our basic Baptist beliefs. I know some will say, "I was a Baptist born; I was a Baptist bred; and when I die, I will be a Baptist dead." Well, you may be, but it would be nice if you could be informed and know our Baptist distinctives.

I want us to begin a pilgrimage together through these pages to discover, rediscover, reaffirm, or remind ourselves again what have been our Baptist distinctives and heritage through the past centuries. Our distinctives are the beliefs that distinguish Baptists from other Christians. Honestly, I am reluctant to write about Baptist distinctives. Why? I do not want to contribute further to the narrowness that is already so prevalent within our denomination today. I see myself as part and product of the wider Christian community. I serve not only as a Baptist on our local association, state, and national levels, but I also labor alongside other Christians in ecumenical efforts. We Baptists share much in common with other Christians, and we should labor for the unity of the church for which our Lord prayed.

OUR WIDER IDENTITY

One of our great Baptist theologians was Walter Rauschenbusch. He concluded his article, "Why I Am a Baptist," with an insight I would like to use as a preface to my comments about our Baptist beliefs.

> I should do harm if I gave Baptists the impression that "we are the people and that there are no others." We are not a perfect denomination. We are capable of being just as narrow and small as anybody. There are fine qualities in which other denominations surpass us. I do not want to foster Baptist self-conceit, because thereby I should grieve the Spirit of Christ. I do not want to make Baptists shut themselves up in their little clam shells and be indifferent to the ocean outside of them. I am a Baptist, but I am more than a Baptist. All things are mine; whether Francis of Assisi, or Luther, or Knox, or Wesley; all are mine because I am Christ's. The old Adam is a strict denominationalist; the new Adam is just a Christian.[1]

I share that quote with you at the beginning of this study with hopes that you will remember our wider identity as I write about what I think are our Baptist distinctives. I always want us to remember that we are part of a larger Christian community. But we do need to know our distinguishing Baptist beliefs. First Peter 3:15 reminds us, "Always be ready to make your defense to anyone who demands from you an accounting for the hope that is in you." Unfortunately, many of us could not begin to tell others why we are Christians and, in particular, why we are Baptists.

Kenneth Scott Latourette, who taught at Yale for many years, was an internationally famous church historian. Someone asked him one time why he was a Baptist. "I am a Baptist," he replied, "by inheritance, inertia, and conviction." Well, a lot of us are Baptists because we inherited our church. Our parents took us to a Baptist church when we were children, and we have simply continued on that path. Some of us are Baptists because of inertia. We simply have not moved out of the Baptist church where we started. We are still within the familiar Baptist doors. But I would like to think that we could remain Baptists because we have convictions that enable us to understand our distinguishing beliefs.

MY BAPTIST ROOTS

I am not a stranger or a newcomer to the Baptist denomination. When I was a small child, my parents started taking me to a Baptist church in Virginia that was not far from where we lived. When I was sixteen years old, I made a profession of faith and became a Christian in that Baptist church. The next year I was youth week pastor in our church.

The following year I was asked to serve again as youth week pastor. I preached a youth revival Sunday through Saturday night in my home church during my senior year in high school. Can you imagine what brilliance I shared with my listeners in those sermons? Though I was young and inexperienced, this congregation was composed of patient, loving, and affirming Christians. They later licensed me to preach before I left for college.

I attended Bluefield Junior College to begin studying for the ministry. While I was at Bluefield, I preached several youth revivals and supplied whenever I had an opportunity. I was elected youth week pastor twice in my college church during my first and second years of study. Following my first year in college, I served as a summer missionary to California. After my second year, I went as a summer missionary to Hawaii. I was the Baptist Student Union president at Bluefield College, and in my senior year I was BSU president at the University of Richmond, where I completed my college education. While at the University of Richmond, I worked during the week at a Baptist Goodwill Mission Center in downtown Richmond.

I was called as pastor of my first church when I was a junior at the University of Richmond. The members of Good Hope Baptist Church were gracious, loving people and helped nurture and care for me in my growth as a minister. I graduated from a Baptist junior college, a Baptist senior college, and the Southeastern Baptist Theological Seminary in North Carolina, and then received my Doctor of Theology degree from the New Orleans Baptist Theological Seminary. Later, I taught for five years at The Southern Baptist Theological Seminary. I have served as a trustee and as a member of a number of committees and boards on the associational and state levels in Baptist life. I have also served in the Baptist World Alliance.

For more than forty years, I have been affiliated with Baptists. I am no stranger to the Baptist way of life nor some newcomer on the Baptist block. I grew up going to a Baptist Sunday school and Training Union. I attended Baptist camps, retreats, revivals, and other meetings in which I was exposed to what Baptists believe. I know what Baptists believe because I have been taught those beliefs at every place I have ever been. I make no apology for declaring that I know something about what Baptists believe. I have had those beliefs crammed down my throat and ears and into my mind all of my life.

Join me on this pilgrimage as I share with you some of our basic Baptist beliefs.

A REGENERATE CHURCH MEMBERSHIP

Our first distinctive as Baptists is the declaration that we believe in a regenerate church membership. What is a regenerate church membership? A regenerate church is one where every member of the church is a Christian. He or she at some point has made a profession of faith in Christ as Lord and has been saved by grace.

Baptists have historically demanded a regenerate church membership. E. Y. Mullins stated in *The Axioms of Religion* that "the ecclesiastical significance of Baptists is a regenerated church membership."[2] One of our oldest Baptist confessions of faith, dated August 10, 1656, affirmed this view: "That in admitting of members into the church of Christ, it is the duty of the church, and ministers whom it concerns, in faithfulness to God, that they be careful they receive none but such as do make forth evident demonstration of a new birth, and the work of faith with power."[3] This position was also affirmed in the Philadelphia (1743, 1798) and Charleston (1774) Confessions. J. B. Jeter, one of the Baptist religious leaders in Virginia, wrote in about 1876, "A spiritual or regenerate church membership lies at the foundation of all Baptist peculiarities."[4] There is no question that historically Baptists have declared that personal religious experience is essential.

What does the emphasis on regenerate church membership mean? It places religious experience at the center of our faith. Only people who are Christians are supposed to be members of our churches. Luke describes the nature of those who were members of the first church in these words: "And day by day the Lord added to their number those who were saved" (Acts 2:47). He adds, "Yet more than ever *believers* were added to the Lord, great numbers of men and women" (Acts 5:14). Paul, in writing to the young churches, addresses them as the "saints." In one letter he writes, "To the church of God that is in Corinth, to those who are sanctified in Christ Jesus, called to be saints" (1 Cor 1:2). Who were the saints? Were they special or unusually holy people who had halos encircling their heads? No. Saints were Christians. Anyone who has been saved by God's grace is a saint. The church is supposed to be composed of Christians who have committed their lives to Christ.

This means religious experience is absolutely essential to church membership. We are unapologetically an evangelistic people. We proclaim that before a person can be a member of a Baptist congregation, he or she must encounter Jesus Christ as Lord. Before one becomes a church member, that person has to undergo a new birth or a re-creation. Experiential religion is central to us. An experience of God's grace is foundational. Each individual is called to an encounter with God. No one is automatically born a Christian. Each individual must make this personal decision. No one is supposed to be a member of a Baptist church who has not been saved by grace. Some critics are quick to say, "Well, that may be the theory, but when I look at Baptist churches, I don't see much evidence that all these people have been saved by grace." I have to confess that this criticism often seems valid.

I heard about a young girl who was visiting a relative. As she watched her aunt put cold cream on her face one night, she asked, "Auntie, what are you doing?"

"Oh, I am making myself beautiful," the aunt replied.

A few minutes later, when she saw her aunt wipe the cold cream off her face, the little girl said to her aunt, "Didn't work, did it?"

Some people look at Baptist churches who claim that their members are regenerated and say, "It didn't work, did it? We don't see the evidence of changed lives in your churches."

We do not have perfect churches. Unfortunately, we may have many people in our churches who have never truly experienced God's grace. But that is not our intention. We seek to reach out to men and women and bring them into a saving knowledge of Jesus Christ as Lord.

The first disciples began with a great claim: "I know whom I have believed." In the small epistle of 1 John the writer says, "That which we have seen with our eyes, that which we have heard with our ears, that which we have handled with our hands, we declare unto you" (1:1-2). At stake was a personal experience with the living Christ.

Vitality in the church does not come by proxy or by someone living on another's experience. A vital church is built on individuals who have their own dynamic relationship with the Lord of the church. Our faith is supposed to be personal, just as the early disciples had a personal experience with Christ. Granted, we cannot go back and walk with the living Christ along the shores of Galilee, but Jesus Christ needs to be a real presence for us today. Our experience should be so real that we sense the power of his presence that changes and transforms us.

PERSONAL EXPERIENCE

The church calls people to a vital religious experience with the living Lord. For someone to become a Christian, that experience must be personal. My relationship to Christ cannot be by proxy. No one else can make my decision to become a Christian for me. It has to be a firsthand experience, not secondhand. It has to be received by conviction, not compulsion. No one can force another to believe. That decision with Christ has to be free and voluntary.

A person's experience with Christ needs to be an immediate one. I have to declare my faith. I have to acknowledge the recognition of my sins and my repentance. Nobody else can repent for me or for you. Parents, friends, or relatives cannot make that decision for another person. They can pray, "This my child is a sinner, save him, O God." But each individual has to declare his or her own sins before God and request God's grace.

Many pastors and professors conduct tours. I thought of a tour group I could organize. I might call it "Tuck's Back to God Tour." We might see if we could go back to places where people say they have experienced God. We would go back and try to find the place where Abraham was willing to go searching for a city that was without foundation. We would try to find the place where Jacob experienced the angels ascending and descending a ladder before God. We would try to find the remains of the bush that was burning where Moses had an experience with God. We would try to discover the ruins of the temple where Isaiah saw God high and lifted up. We would try to find the footprints in the sand where the disciples followed Jesus as they left their nets to become fishers of men. We would try to find the place on the Damascus Road where Paul had his blinding experience with Christ. We would move on down through history and see if we could find the garden spot where Augustine heard the voice saying, "Take up and read," and he himself was converted. We would climb the stairs in Rome where Luther searched to find the Spirit of God. We could go to Aldersgate where Wesley's heart was "strangely warmed."

But there are several problems with that kind of tour. For one thing, we probably cannot find those spots. The biggest problem, though, is that such a tour focuses on the past. We seem to think that we must go back someplace and find out what God did for somebody in the past. The angel said to those who came to the tomb searching for Jesus, "You seek Jesus of Nazareth, but he is not here. . . . He has gone before you" (Matt 28:6, 7). Christ is always going before his church seeking to draw us into the future. He is not content with what we have been or where we have been.

The Lord is not confined to the past. He goes before us to meet us in the present here and now. We worship not a dead Lord but a living Lord who seeks to meet us at every corner of life. When we encounter this living Christ, we experience a new birth and are recreated through that personal encounter.

We Baptists affirm experiential religion. Salvation comes about by God's grace. Grace is *our* undeserved love from God. Grace is God's *unconditional* love. We are saved not because of our works or deeds, but by grace. This is indeed marvelous news, as John Newton, the composer of "Amazing Grace," wrote. He himself was a living testimony to the radical change grace can bring in life.

By grace *you* are saved. Each of us is redeemed by God. This doctrine proclaims the primacy of the individual and the voluntary nature of faith. A regenerate church stresses the significance of "soul competency." Each person is called to make his or her response to God.

A number of years ago Carlyle Marney spoke at New Orleans Baptist Theological Seminary, lecturing in chapel in vintage Marney style. When he finished, to be perfectly honest, almost no one knew what he had said. Marney often spoke in a heavy, theologically abstract manner. Following his lecture, he was invited to one of the seminary classrooms to answer questions. A new student in the class had not learned to be theologically "cool" and pretend that he knew what had been said when he didn't. "Dr. Marney," he said, "I didn't have the foggiest notion what you were talking about today. Could you tell us in some clear statement what you were trying to say?" Dr. Marney peered over his glasses at that young man as if he was going to stare a hole the size of the Grand Canyon through him. Then he got up and walked over to the blackboard and wrote these words: "GOD IS FOR YOU." And he underlined *you*.[5]

God is for *you*. God is for each of us. For by grace *you* have been saved. You have been saved from the power and tyranny of sin, from your burden of guilt, and from your past. You have been saved by the grace of God through faith. Faith is the small footbridge over the chasm of uncertainty. You are saved by faith, not by works. Salvation is not by some action you do with hand, body, or mind. By grace you are saved through faith.

AFFIRMING GRACE ONLY

I find it astonishing to hear Baptists who want to add something else to God's grace! Some say we have to have more than faith to become Christians. These people say that to become a Christian, you have to believe not only in Christ but in the inerrancy of the Scriptures, in the plenary substitution theory of the atonement, or other doctrines. I do not hear the New Testament saying that. "By grace you are saved through faith" (Eph 2:8). I hear the New Testament saying, "Believe on the Lord Jesus Christ and you will be saved" (Acts 16:31).

Attempts to add other items to salvation turn it into works righteousness. This becomes an invention of a man or woman as each tries to add to God's grace. Ancient heresies die hard. All attempts to redefine salvation by grace and add to it represent a new version of the ancient gnostic heresy. This effort to add "secret" theological beliefs to God's grace is a denial of our basic distinctives of personal religious experience based on faith in God's grace.

To become a Christian does not demand that a person have the full knowledge of Christian doctrine or beliefs. The disciples of Jesus began to follow him before they fully understood what his call meant. As a lad of sixteen, did I understand what I think I comprehend about God now? Of course not! Faith is not assenting to a long list of theological propositions. We are not summoned to believe in a long list of doctrines about God or Christ. We are summoned to "believe in Christ." Faith is personal, not propositional. No one can make up a long list of doctrines we must believe before we can become a Christian.

Robert Raines was putting his young son to bed once when the boy looked up at him and said, "Daddy, tell me again, what does Maundy Thursday mean?" In their church tradition, they were celebrating a special service on the Thursday before Easter. Dr. Raines told his child that Maundy Thursday was the night Jesus had his last meal with his disciples. Raines explained that while the disciples and Jesus ate together, Jesus talked to them about what the meal symbolized. The father told his son that Jesus left the upper room, later was crucified on Good Friday, and then was raised from the dead by God. He said we celebrate Easter because of the great event of the resurrection of Christ. Then the young son looked at his father and asked, "Daddy, will Easter ever happen to me?" The church is supposed to be composed of those who claim they have experienced Easter. Easter has to happen to each of us as we commit our lives to Jesus Christ as the living Lord.

THE VARIETY OF CONVERSION EXPERIENCES

We do not all have to have the same kind of conversion experience. We will not all become Christians in exactly the same way. Can we expect a nine-year-old child to have the same kind of understanding about Christ that a sixteen-year-old, a thirty-year old, or a forty-year-old has? There is a different level of response for each person—girl, boy, woman, man. But as we each respond out of our own awareness, each still experiences God's wonderful grace.

For some people, conversion is a radically emotional experience. Then there are others like Ruth Graham, the wife of the famous evangelist, Billy Graham, who honestly stated that she could not remember when she became a Christian. Mrs. Graham grew up in the home of a minister and could never remember not feeling close to God. But she knew that at some point, she quietly surrendered her life to God.

Each experience with God can be different. Some of us may identify with the experience of W. T. Conner. He said a number of people talked to him at what was then called the "mourner's bench." He went up to the front of his church and knelt and prayed. But somehow or another it was not much help to him. It only made his decision more difficult, he said. One day, he said, he finally gave up. When he gave up, his burden was removed. Connor said, "I didn't have any great feeling of ecstatic joy. I did not feel like shouting or anything. I simply felt that my burden was gone and I hardly knew what had happened."[6] Later, this man would become one of our great Baptist theologians and teach at Southwestern Baptist Theological Seminary.

John Sampey was president of Southern Seminary and, for a while, president of the Southern Baptist Convention at the same time. When he was young, Sampey had no peace in his heart. He could not shake off his burden of sin. No one could tell him what he needed to do to get rid of that burden. He lay in his bed on the night of March 3, 1877, and could not sleep. He later gave the following account:

In desperation I lifted my eyes up and began to talk in a whisper to the Saviour. I said to Him, "Lord, Jesus, I do not know what to do. I have prayed, but I get no relief. . . . I have read the Bible, but my sins are still a burden on my soul. I have listened to preaching, but I can find no help. I do not know what to do except turn it all over to you. And if I am lost I will go down trusting you." Then something happened. It seemed that a great presence filled the room, and said to me almost in audible words, "My boy, I have been waiting for you to do what you have just done. You can count on me to save you. I will not fail you." My pillow was wet with tears of joy that Christ Jesus was now my personal Saviour![7]

God's Spirit works in a variety of ways in the human heart.

BELIEVER'S BAPTISM

Because Baptists believe in a regenerate church membership, we baptize only believers. We do not baptize infants, because a child is passive. A parent cannot make a faith decision for someone else. We do not believe in baptismal regeneration. We believe that baptism is a sign or a symbol that the person being baptized is already regenerated. A person who has committed his or her life to Christ on a profession of faith is baptized, as Paul says in Romans 6:3, "into the death of Christ." Being lowered under the baptismal waters denotes radical identification with Christ's suffering and death and the desire to follow him. "I am crucified with Christ" is the way Paul states it elsewhere. From the baptismal waters, we are raised up to walk in newness of life with Christ.

Baptists believe that immersion is the means of baptism that best testifies to the New Testament image of conversion. In all serious, scholarly studies, no evidence is found for sprinkling until the second century. Karl Barth, a Lutheran and one of the most renowned theologians of all times, dropped a theological gauntlet before the church when he affirmed that believer's baptism, like the Baptist practice of baptism, is the correct pattern. He called for the rest of the Christian church to acknowledge its error and repent.[8] Infant baptism, Barth said, is based on a slim thread.[9] The places in Acts where one reads that a whole household was baptized also include in most passages that they "all" expressed ecstatic joy. Could an infant respond that way? We baptize by immersion because we believe it is the New Testament symbol that best depicts those who are regenerate within the church of Christ.

A CHRISTIAN LIFESTYLE

We also believe that those who have been regenerated are called to live responsible lives that bear testimony to Christ. If you and I really are regenerate, then the world should know we are Christians. As Jesus said, "You will know my disciples by their fruits" (Matt 7:16). As Paul says in Romans 6:4, "We were buried with him (Christ) in baptism that we might walk in newness of life." Our lives should give evidence of that faith.

Gordon Kingsley, former president of William Jewell College, liked to tell about an early trustee of that college and a signer of the college's charter, the Reverend Robert James. He had two notorious sons, Jesse and Frank, who never attended the college—fortunately, Dr. Kingsley likes to say. After their father's death, each son donated $26.50 to pay off the pledge their father had made to the college as a trustee. Shortly after Jesse had robbed the banks at Liberty; Lexington; Richmond, Missouri; and Russellville, Kentucky; he was baptized in the Kearney Baptist Church where his father was pastor. Following his baptism, he robbed the bank at Gallatin, Missouri. His pious mother was pleased that he had been "converted."

That story is true. One of the stories about Jesse, which may be fact or fiction, is about a time when Jesse, Frank, and some "colaborers" were robbing a train. As Jesse walked down the aisle, he extended his hat to a Baptist deacon who was wearing a black frock coat and stove pipe hat. But he received only 36 cents from this prosperous-looking fellow. Thinking that this gentleman could give more than he had given, Jesse put the revolver against the man's head and asked if he did not have more money. The deacon answered in truth that he did have $18.12 in his boot, but that it had been collected by the pious people of his congregation to give to a missionary cause and he felt he did not want to betray the pious people of his Baptist church who had given so sacrificially. Upon hearing the name Baptist, Jesse took the revolver out of his right hand and placed it in his left hand, then reached down and said: "Shake, brother, I'm a Baptist too!"[10]

Unfortunately, we have a lot of folks like Jesse James who may be on a church roll but are not regenerate. They may have been baptized, but that does not mean they are Christian. Being baptized or walking down an aisle does not automatically, hocus pocus-style, make you or me a Christian.

11

Those who have been regenerated by the power of Christ will show some demonstration of that conversion in their lives.

An apple tree produces apples because it is an apple tree. The fruit comes from the nature of the tree. Those of us who have truly met Christ and have been transformed by his grace will live lives that demonstrate to the world that we are truly regenerated. I pray that all people will be able to see by our living that each of us has actually experienced the power of God's grace.

NOTES

[1] Walter Rauschenbusch, "Why I Am a Baptist," *A Baptist Treasury*, comp. Sydnor L. Stealey (New York: Thomas Y. Crowell Co., 1958), 183-84.

[2] E. Y. Mullins, *The Axioms of Religion* (Philadelphia: Judson Press, 1908), 56-57.

[3] W. L. Lumpkin, *Baptist Confessions of Faith* (Philadelphia: Judson Press, 1908), 56-57.

[4] Jeremiah B. Jeter, *Baptist Principles Reset* (Richmond: Religious Herald Co., 1902), 18.

[5] Walter B. Shurden, *The Doctrine of the Priesthood of Believers* (Nashville: Convention Press, 1987), 45.

[6] Stewart A. Newman, *W. T. Conner: Theologian of the Southwest* (Nashville: Broadman Press, 1964), 73.

[7] John R. Sampey, *Memoirs of John R. Sampey* (Nashville: Broadman Press,1947), 6-7.

[8] Karl Barth, *The Teaching of the Church Regarding Baptism* (London: SCM Press, 1963), 40f., 49.

[9] Ibid., 44ff.

[10] Gordon Kingsley, "On Swallowing the Gos-Pill," *Light* (January-February 1983): 4.

CHAPTER TWO

A Non-creedal People

Suppose you came by my study this week and told me you wanted to become a Christian. You felt you had had a vital and life-changing experience with God, and you wanted to make a commitment of faith to God. Suppose I said to you, "I recognize that is a very momentous decision. You need to understand carefully what you are doing. Let me state clearly what you must believe to be a Christian. You must affirm the following."

> [I] believe in one God the Father All-sovereign, maker of all things visible and invisible; And in one Lord Jesus Christ, the Son of God, begotten of the Father, only-begotten, that is, of the substance of the Father, God of God, Light of Light, true God of true God, begotten not made, of one substance with the Father, through whom all things were made, things in heaven and things on the earth; who for us men and for our salvation came down and was made flesh, and became man, suffered, and rose on the third day, ascended into the heavens, is coming to judge living and dead.

And in the Holy Spirit.

And those that say "There was when he was not,"

and, "Before he was begotten he was not,"

and that, "He came into being from what-is-not,"

or those that allege, that the Son of God is

"Of another substance or essence"

or "created,"

or "changeable"

or "alterable,"

these the Catholic and Apostolic Church anathematizes.[1]

"Do you believe this?" I would then ask. "Can you say you understand and affirm this statement? If so, you can become a Christian."

I just quoted one of the historical creeds of the church, the Creed of Nicaea. This is the version revised by the ancient church historian Eusebius and is one of the historic creeds of the church that has been passed down through the centuries. Many statements in the creed are marvelous, wonderful declarations about God. But these statements are so philosophical, abstract, and impersonal that most people today cannot begin to grasp them. This creed was written originally to address a particular theological controversy that had arisen in the fourth century church.

THE PURPOSE OF CREEDS

Creeds or confessions of faith have their place in the life of the church. Creeds or confessions may have begun primarily for missionary purposes of the church. They were formulated to explain to unbelievers what Christians believed. They were used in an apologetic way to witness to the faith. It was a way to testify to what the Christians "had seen and heard." In Acts, Luke pointed to Paul's Damascus road experience, and Paul confessed his faith through his epistles to the new Gentile churches. Creeds were also used as teaching tools. They usually gave a summary or a digest of the Christian faith. Sometimes they presented a summary of the basic facts about the life, ministry, death, and resurrection of Christ. Creeds were often used at the time a person was baptized. Before a person was baptized and accepted as a member of the church, he or she was asked to confess certain creedal statements. Creeds were later formulated to denounce heresy and affirm the orthodox faith, but this was not their original purpose.

Creeds have always had their limitations and inadequacies. Even those who follow creedal traditions acknowledge the limitations of creeds. Alan Richardson, who was Canon of Durham, England, and Professor of Christian Theology in the University of Nottingham, made the following observation in his book *Creeds in the Making*:

> The realization that the essence of the Christian religion is belief in a person rather than in a doctrine or system of ideas explains why doctrines must be reformulated for every generation, and why no particular system of doctrine can ever be final. Every age must make afresh its own interpretation of the central fact of history.[2]

Every generation must refocus, deepen, expand, interpret, and understand any creedal or confessional statement. I do not believe such statements can be finalized for future generations.

One of the reasons creedal statements arose in the first place in the early church was to enable the disciples to explain their experiences with the risen Lord. The resurrection of Jesus was the transforming fact in the life of the disciples and was one of the first beliefs to which they attested. "Christ is risen," they proclaimed. Paul described the call to repentance this way: "If you confess with your lips that Jesus is Lord and believe in your heart that God raised him from the dead, you will be saved" (Rom 10:9).

The apostle Paul expressed his belief in the incarnation and redemption of Christ, as the other apostles did, in the language and religious images of the first century. Paul drew on ideas from his time to express the truth about the incarnation of Christ. In Philippians 2:9, Paul used the Greek word *kenosis*, which means "self-emptying." This Greek word for "emptied" pictures something being poured out of a container into something else. Theologians have debated for centuries what Paul meant by that word. The readers in his day likely understood its meaning. But those of us who have been separated from its original intent by centuries find the language obscure and difficult to grasp. Generations later, Christians have to express that truth in ways that are meaningful to us today. Karl Barth has reminded us that "the life of the Church is not exhausted by confessing its faith."[3] No one can ever state theological insights of one generation as though they were the final way of expressing the ultimate truth about God.

Creeds and confessions have meaning if we can see the intention behind them. We need to ask ourselves: "What truths are they seeking to expound?

Is their goal a missionary intention, a summary of the faith, or an attempt to clarify Christian beliefs?" The renowned German theologian Wolfhart Pannenberg, who comes from a tradition that uses creeds, states:

> The formulations of the Apostles' Creed are the summing up of the sustaining foundations of the faith, which also form its central content. They speak in the language of their time, which can no longer be in every respect our language. . . . Most people would no longer of their own accord formulate many statements in the Apostles' Creed as they stand. In spite of that, we can still repeat the creed in church without doing violence to our personal sincerity as long as we are able to adhere to the *intention behind its statements*, critical though we may be of the form these statements may take.[4] (Italics mine)

What is Pannenberg saying? He is reminding us that we have got to get behind creedal statements to sense the intentions of those who composed them. We do not have to accept them literally or assume they have expressed the truth of the faith in the only way possible for every generation.

When I was on a sabbatical leave from St. Matthews Baptist Church in Louisville, Kentucky, my wife Emily and I had the privilege of worshiping daily at Christ Church Cathedral in Oxford, England, a historical Anglican church. Worship there was always a deeply moving experience for us. One of the traditional parts of most of the worship services was a recitation of the Apostles' Creed. I want to confess that I freely recited the Apostles' Creed in those services of worship. How could I do that as a Baptist? Because I understood the intention behind the Apostles' Creed. I did not believe that this verbal expression of the faith was binding me theologically to the exact words of this ancient creed. I knew, of course, that this creed did not originate with the apostles, nor was it the oldest creedal expression of the Christian faith. I recognized that it was clothed in the language and thought of another age. The Apostles' Creed is based on the old Roman Creed, which is dated to the middle of the fourth century. The form as it is recited today is more than a thousand years old. I may not always agree with its ancient way of expressing the Christian faith, but I agree with the intention behind it.

Theological statements, nevertheless, are important. The word *theology* means "a study about God." We devote a lot of time studying theology in churches. Our seminaries and colleges teach courses on theology and the

Bible. As Christians, we all want to learn as much as we can about God, Christ, the Holy Spirit, the Scriptures, creation, the atonement, and other doctrines. As the Westminster Confession proclaims, we long "to know God and enjoy him forever." The reason we gather for Sunday school and worship is to understand and love God more completely.

THE INCOMPLETENESS OF THEOLOGICAL STATEMENTS

But as Baptists, we affirm that no theological statement is ever final or complete. No one person or group of people can formulate our theology for us and say that this is what we have to believe. Our forefathers and mothers have fought and died for this free tradition. One of the reasons no theological statement can be made absolute is that much religious language is symbolic. How can anyone finalize a theological statement about God when our knowledge is always partial, inadequate, or incomplete?

We state that God is personal. What does that mean? God is obviously not a person like I am a person. To describe God as personal does not limit God to a person. We often pray to God as Father. Does that image mean God is male? God is surely not limited by our human image of a man. As Spirit, God transcends all sexuality. God is not bound by human sexuality. As Creator, God would incorporate the essence of all sexuality but not be limited by it. God cannot be confined to any of our human images or descriptions. Who dares to say that he or she has described God fully and has exhausted the images of God's nature? That would be an arrogant assumption on the part of any person.

Who understands fully the mystery of the atoning work of Christ? Look for a moment at Paul's theories about the atonement. Occasionally, I hear someone say we have to believe in a certain view of the atonement as the only interpretation. This is often presented as the substitutionary theory. I believe the substitutionary view of the atonement is taught in the Scriptures. But Paul uses numerous other images to try to explain the death of Christ. He drew these images from the law court, the accounting ledger, the family, the slave market, the Jewish sacrificial system, and other places. No one image was final or conveyed all Paul wanted to say. I wonder sometimes if even Paul really understood all that was involved in the atonement. He himself confessed the mystery of Christ's death. Do we dare to say that Paul has the only and final understanding or interpretation of the atonement? Paul did not exhaust the mystery of the atonement. We have the interpretations of John, Mark, Matthew, Luke, and other New Testament writers. We are constantly seeking to grasp and understand the meaning of the atonement. "One utter heresy in Christianity," Harry Emerson Fosdick wrote, "is thus to believe that we have reached finality and can settle down with a completed system."[5]

Seminary students give various reactions as they try to wrestle with contemporary theological insights. Some seminary wag drew a cartoon that pictured Jesus talking to Simon Peter at Caesarea Philippi. Peter responded to the first question, "Who do men say that the Son of Man is?" And then he replied to the question, "But who do you say that I am?" Peter answered, "Thou art the paradoxical Kerygma, the epistemological manifestation of the existential ground of ontological ultimacy."

Jesus responded simply, "Huh?"

What am I saying? We need to study ancient and contemporary theologians, be familiar with philosophical and theological language, and be aware of how we got our Bible and how scholars interpret it. But remember that no single theological interpretation can ever be regarded as final and complete for all future generations. Every generation has the challenge and responsibility to understand and define theological statements about God for its own generation. Christ is changeless, but we will always describe him in changing categories.

THE RADICAL NATURE OF THE GOSPEL

We Baptists are non-creedal people. Why? This conviction is rooted in the radical nature of the gospel that Jesus proclaimed. In Mark's Gospel, Jesus used an image familiar to the Jewish people of his day to describe the radical nature of his kingdom. He reminded them about the necessity for having new wineskins to preserve new wine. In ancient times, fresh wine was usually poured into animal skins for storage. As long as the skin was new, it was flexible and could expand as the wine fermented. But if the skins were old, dry, and brittle and someone poured new wine into them, they would explode or break and the wine would be lost. "Fresh skins for new wine" (Mark 2:22).

The gospel Jesus announced was so radical that it would break all traditions and barriers. The kingdom of God is so fresh that it has to have new forms and shapes. It cannot be fenced in. The Pharisees tried to preserve the old wineskins. The message of Jesus exploded the old wineskins that tried to exclude women, sinners, the outcast, and the unclean from his kingdom.

The old wineskins exploded when the religious leaders tried to exclude the publicans and tax collectors. Jesus ate with them and called them to be his disciples. Jesus exploded the old wineskins about the traditions of fasting and Sabbath observance. He often broke the Sabbath law! Old wineskins burst. Jesus described a kingdom so radical that no systems could confine or contain it. Paul described it in these words: "The old has passed away, behold the new has come" (2 Cor 5:17).

Acts 15 tells about a quarrel in the early church. This quarrel was an attempt by a group of Judaizers to keep the gospel in old wineskins. Paul had gone to churches at Antioch, Cilicia, and Syria, and some of the Gentiles in these communities had become Christians. But when the Judaizers came from Jerusalem, they demanded that these people be circumcised if they wanted to become Christians. They demanded that the Gentile converts keep the Jewish traditions. Paul argued against the Judaizers. The problem became so intense in the churches that a conference was held in Jerusalem to resolve it. If the Judaizers had been successful, Christianity would have become merely a sect of Judaism and soon might have disappeared. The conference decided that the Gentile believers did not have to keep the ancient Jewish tradition of circumcision or follow the Torah. They were encouraged to live by high moral standards that would distinguish them from the pagans.

Thank goodness Christianity was not limited to the traditions of Judiasm! This was a crucial point in the history of the young church. Fortunately, Paul prevailed. This victory broke through old wineskins. John Broadus summed up well the problem with Judaizers: "They always exaggerate the importance of externals."[6] Judaizers always try to keep the gospel in old wineskins. They have never grasped the radical nature of God's kingdom.

BAPTIST OPPOSITION TO CREEDS

Judaizers are still at work. We feel the impact of them in our Baptist life today. They want to confine the faith to old wineskins of their own design. When any person or group attempts to finalize our beliefs by their rigid interpretations, they have become Judaizers. In the preface to his source book, *Baptist Confessions of Faith*, William L. Lumpkin reminds Baptists, "For them confessions have never been simply manifestos of prevailing doctrine in particular groups. No confession has ever permanently bound individuals, churches, associations, conventions, or unions among Baptists."[7]

When the Southern Baptist Convention was formed in 1845, this statement was issued by its first president, W. B. Johnson: "We have constructed for our basis no new creed, acting in this matter upon a Baptist aversion for all creeds but the Bible."[8] The conveners further clarified their reason for forming this new denomination in the words of the preamble to their constitution. The conveners intended to provide "a plan for eliciting, combining, and directing the energies of the denomination for the propagation of the gospel."[9] Why did we come together originally as Southern Baptists? It was solely for the purpose of missions. We wanted to reach other people for Christ. Dr. H. Leon McBeth, one of our Baptist historians, has stated this truth in these lines:

> The famed Southern Baptist unity in the past has been more functional than theological; Southern Baptists have banned together to minister in missions, evangelism, and Christian education. So long as they emphasize functional ministry, the "rope of sand," as one called it, holds; when they switch from function to doctrine, unity is threatened.[10]

As Baptists, we have never believed creeds should be imposed upon others. In the confession of faith by Southern Baptists, written in 1962 and titled *The Baptist Faith and Message*, the preamble states clearly:

> Baptists are a people who profess a living faith. This faith is rooted and grounded in Jesus Christ who is "the same yesterday, today, and forever." Therefore, the sole authority for faith and practice among Baptists is Jesus Christ whose will is revealed in the Holy Scriptures.
>
> A living faith must experience a growing understanding of truth and must be continually interpreted and related to the needs of each new generation. Throughout their history Baptist bodies, both large and small, have issued statements of faith which comprise a consensus of their beliefs. *Such statements have never been regarded as complete, infallible statements of faith, nor as official creeds carrying mandatory authority.*[11] (Italics mine)

The Peace Committee's report, adopted at the annual meeting of the Southern Baptist Convention in 1987, states clearly that same truth in the following words:

> We must never try to impose upon individual Southern Baptists nor local congregations a specific view of how Scripture must be interpreted. If such an attempt is made, then reconciliation is not the goal, nor is it possible to achieve. . . . Baptists are non-creedal, in that they do not impose a man-made interpretation of Scripture on others.[12]

On June 14, 2000, the Southern Baptist Convention adopted a revised summary of the Southern Baptist faith. The committee's report stated in part:

> Baptists cherish and defend religious liberty, and deny the right of any secular or religious authority to impose a confession of faith upon a church or body of churches. We honor the principles of soul competency and the priesthood of believers, affirming together both our liberty in Christ and our accountability to each other under the Word of God. (Introductory statement in the *2000 Baptist Faith and Message*)

Having made that statement, the committee said that they wanted to identify and affirm "certain definite doctrines that Baptists believe, cherish, and with which they have been and are now closely identified." Added to the summary paragraph about religious liberty, soul competency, and the priesthood believers is the following strong assertion:

> Baptist churches, associations, and general bodies have adopted confessions of faith as a witness to the world, and as instruments of doctrinal accountability. We are not embarrassed to state before the world that these are doctrines we hold precious and as essential to the Baptist tradition of faith and practice. (Preamble of the *2000 Baptist Faith and Message*)

Rather than granting fellow Baptists their freedom of soul competency, the *2000 Baptist Faith and Message* became the criterion by which one was judged to be an "authentic" Baptist. If you differed with any part of it, such as the removal of the sentence in *I. Scripture* that states, "the criterion by which the Bible is to be interpreted is Jesus Christ" (*1963 Baptist Faith and Message*), or the addition in *VI. The Church* that states, "the office of pastor is limited to men as qualified by Scripture" (*2000 Baptist Faith and Message*), you are not acceptable as a Baptist. The 2000 statement of the *Baptist Faith and Message* became a binding confession of faith, and those who refused to sign that they agreed with it were fired. This happened to seminary professors, missionaries, and other denominational workers. The inerrantist group prevailed within the Southern Baptist Convention and made the *2000 Baptist Faith and Message* binding upon Baptists. It became a creed.

Three hundred years ago, Baptists broke away from the established church because they did not want creeds. They did not want anyone dictating to them what they had to believe. Nor do we want conformity of thought today. The attempt to set up a creed and the other intolerable actions by the inerrantists in the Southern Baptist Convention led to the formation of the Cooperative Baptist Fellowship, the Alliance of Baptists, and other such groups who still cherished Baptist freedom of thought.

Throughout our history we have affirmed as Baptists that no group or individual has the right to impose creeds upon other Baptists. We do not believe that creeds passed down from generation to generation are binding upon us today.

As Baptists we have sometimes used affirmations or confessions of faith. Among the most noted historically might be *The Philadelphia Confession* of 1742 and *The New Hampshire Confession* in 1833. William L. Lumpkin listed in his book all the significant Baptist confessions of faith by various Baptist groups, dating from the earliest Anabaptist days up to the 1925 statement of faith. But in each document, by a statement in the preamble or someplace else, Baptists have historically declared that these confessions were not binding.

We believe in a living faith and not one that can be stated in archaic terms that bind all Baptists forever in a creedal straitjacket. No statement about our faith is ever final or complete. We believe in a living faith that is always open to revision by the Holy Spirit. We reject all attempts at doctrinal uniformity or creedal compulsion.

You may have heard about the rancher who bought ten other ranches in Texas and combined them all into one large spread. A man asked the rancher, "What did you name your new ranch?"

"Well," the rancher replied, "I named it the Circle Q, Rambling Brook, Double Bar, Broken Circle, Crooked Creek, Golden Horse Shoe, Lazy B, Bent Arrow, Sleepy T, Triple O Ranch."

"Wow," the man said. "I bet you have a lot of cattle."

"Nope," said the Texan.

"Why not?" the inquirer asked.

"Not many survive the branding," the owner replied.

When we try to brand each other and say that other people have to agree with our interpretation or they are not Baptists, then we have moved a long way from what it is to be an authentic Baptist. This always creates chaos and dissention. Let's stop branding each other and affirm our differences. I urge us to rejoice in one another and accept one another and be thankful for our diversity. It is a part of our strength and vitality.

The Reasons Baptists Are Opposed to Creeds

Why are we as Baptists a non-creedal people? First of all, because we believe a personal experience with Jesus Christ is foundational for our faith. This experience may be different for every person. When Jesus called his disciples, he didn't give them a long list of beliefs to which they had to ascribe. What did he say to them? "Come, follow me." When the disciples first began to follow Jesus, they didn't begin to understand fully who he was. But they followed him and grew in their awareness of who he was and what he taught. Most of us, when we began our pilgrimage with Jesus Christ, did not fully understand what that commitment of faith meant. But we have continued to grow in our knowledge of Christ and his teachings. This is part of the meaning of sanctification and why we have Christian education in our churches.

Secondly, we believe faith is personal and not propositional. When I meet God, truth is revealed in that experience. But truth is different from a list of truths about God (like the ones set forth in the Nicene Creed) that I must believe. Even the statement "God is love" may be seen as a propositional statement, but I don't understand it like I do two times two equals four. The love of God is something I have to experience or it doesn't have any meaning for me. "Jesus is Lord" may be a propositional statement, but that statement has no meaning unless Jesus Christ is one whom I have experienced as Lord. A person can believe a lot of propositions about God or the Bible and not really believe in God or really use the Bible correctly.

Let me give you an example. If you asked me if I knew Felton Spencer, the former basketball center for the University of Louisville who presently plays for the New York Knicks, I might tell you the following: I know that Felton Spencer is seven feet tall. He had a field goal percentage that set a record for seniors at U of L and in the Metro Conference. His career percentage ranked him as all-time number one for U of L. In his last season at U of L, he averaged 14.9 points, made 8.5 rebounds, and blocked 69 shots. In 1990 he was voted the Most Valuable Player along with LaBradford Smith. He was sixth in the overall selection in June 1990 NBA draft and made a five-year deal for eight million dollars to play for the Minnesota Timberwolves in the National Basketball Association. In 1997–1998 he had a season high of 13 rebounds against the Dallas Mavericks. He has appeared in 34 career NBA Playoff games. He has played for 6 NBA teams and is presently the center for the New York Knicks. I know all of these facts about Felton Spencer. But you ask, "Do you know Felton Spencer?" To be honest with you, I would have to say, "I have never met him." Do you see the difference? I can know *all* of these things about Felton Spencer but not *know* Felton Spencer. We can know all kinds of propositions about God, Christ, or the Bible and not truly know God or Christ or understand the Bible.

Thirdly, we are non-creedal people because we believe in the priesthood of believers. That means that you—every single one of you—have the right to be a priest before God and interpret the Scriptures for yourself. As your pastor, I cannot tell you that there is only one way to understand the Bible, Christ, or God. The priesthood of all believers is one of our most prized beliefs.

In 1888 John Clifford, who was a pastor in London, was elected president of the British Baptist Union. At that time the Baptist Union was marked by efforts to impose doctrinal creedalism upon the members of the Union. In his address titled "The Great Forty Years," Clifford noted:

> Even the first friends of Christianity were never agreed as to its whole contents. Living men differ. It is the dead who agree. Poor shattered fragments that we are! Why! truth would have no chance at all upon the earth if each man were nothing but the . . . echo of his fellow. God sets men at different angles to the truth, so that one may see what another cannot. . . . God will not suffer us to get our best beliefs as we do our coats. . . . Give men a ready-made faith, paid for by pen, subscription, or lip affirma-

tion, and it is on them, not in them, on them like a garment, not in them as a life. . . . Give us a Bible about which two opinions are not possible and we treat it as we do the multiplication table, use it for our grossest needs, but never think of it for the splendid hours of spiritual aspirations and redeeming service.[13]

We do not always have to agree to be Baptists. We can agree to disagree and affirm our right to interpret beliefs differently. Our strength is in our diversity as Baptists and not in a uniformity. We need to resist those who call for everyone to believe alike or agree on everything. It will never happen, nor should it. No one Baptist has all the answers or truth for all the rest of us.

Fourthly, we believe in the autonomy of the local church. No group, association, convention, or anyone else can tell us as Baptists exactly how we are supposed to think, interpret our beliefs, or worship. We have the freedom to interpret the Bible for ourselves and worship as we feel led. No other Baptist or group of Baptists anyplace can come here and tell us that we are not Baptists because we don't believe like they do. Every Baptist church is autonomous.

Finally, we believe the Bible is our sufficient guide and ultimate authority for all matters. In chapter 1, I quoted from Walter Rauschenbusch's marvelous article, "Why I Am a Baptist." Note these lines from that same article:

> Baptists have always insisted that they recognize the Bible alone as their sufficient authority for faith and practice. There are, indeed, many Baptists who have tried to use the Bible just as other denominations use their creeds. They have turned the Bible into one huge creed, and practically that meant: "You must believe everything which we think the Bible means and says." They have tried to impose on us their little interpretation of the great Book as the creed to which all good Baptists must cleave.
>
> But fortunately the Bible is totally different from a creed. A creed contains sharply defined and abstract theology; the Bible contains a record of concrete and glowing religious life. A creed addresses itself to the intellect; the Bible appeals to the whole soul and edifies it. A creed tells you what you must believe; the Bible tells you what holy men have believed. A creed is religious philosophy, the Bible is religious history. A creed gives the truth as it looked to one set of clever men at one particular stage

of human history; the Bible gives the truth as it looked to a great number of God-filled men running through many hundreds of years. The strength of a creed is in its uniformity and its tight fit; the beauty of the Bible is in its marvelous variety and richness. A creed imposes a law and binds thought; the Bible imparts a spirit and awakens thought.[14]

As Baptists, our confessions of faith and theological systems serve as guides for us in our knowledge and interpretation of God, Christ, and the Scriptures. We live under the authority of the lordship of Christ as we best understand it in this present time. We follow our Lord, aware that he may always have further light to cast on our pathway and new truth to teach us about his Father, the world, our neighbor, and ourselves. We confess that our religious knowledge, like all knowledge, is partial and incomplete and is in continuous search for deeper and newer insights. Therefore, we refuse to say we have ever arrived spiritually or have the ultimate interpretation about God or the Scriptures. We always give our brother or sister (fellow Christians), or someone of a different religious persuasion or who espouses no faith at all, the right to his or her own religious or non-religious beliefs. We trust Christ who goes before us through the inspiration of the Holy Spirit to have a word for us today. Our theology is not confined to the past but awaits God's word for us today. We bring to our Lord new wineskins and pray for him to fill them with the freshness and joy of his presence.

NOTES

[1] "The Creed of Nicaea," *Documents of the Christian Church*, ed. Henry Bettenson (New York: Oxford University Press, 1956), 36.

[2] Alan Richardson, *Creeds in the Making* (London: SCM Press, 1961), 11. An excellent resource for this study is "Baptist Confessions of Faith," *Review & Expositor* (Winter 1979).

[3] Karl Barth, *Creeds* (New York: Charles Scribner's Sons, 1962), 9.

[4] Wolfhart Pannenberg, *The Apostles Creed* (Philadelphia: Westminster Press, 1972), 13.

[5] Harry Emerson Fosdick, *Adventurous Religion* (New York: Blue Ribbon Books, 1926), 5.

[6] John Broadus, "The Duty of Baptists to Teach Their Distinctive Views," *A Baptist Treasury*, ed. Sydnor L. Stealey (New York: Thomas Y. Crowell Co., 1958), 143.

[7] W. L. Lumpkin, *Baptist Confessions of Faith* (Philadelphia: Judson Press, 1959), 17.

[8] Proceedings of the Southern Baptist Convention, 1845 (Richmond: H. K. Ellyson, 1945), 19.

[9] Ibid. This statement is also found in every yearly report of the Southern Baptist Convention. See the 1989 *SBC Annual* (Nashville: Executive Committee, SBC, 1989), 4.

[10] H. Leon McBeth, *The Baptist Heritage* (Nashville: Broadman Press, 1987), 685.

[11] *The Baptist Faith and Message* (Nashville: Sunday School Board of the Southern Baptist Convention, 1963), 5.

[12] Report of the Southern Baptist Convention Peace Committee, 15, 16.

[13] John Clifford, "The Great Forty Years," *A Baptist Treasury*, ed. S. L. Stealey (New York: Thomas Crowell Co., 1956), 97-102.

[14] Walter Rauschenbusch, "Why I Am a Baptist," *A Baptist Treasury*, ed. S. L. Stealey (New York: Thomas Crowell Co., 1958), 181-82.

CHAPTER THREE

The Authority of Scripture

In the delightful book titled *Children's Letters to God*, a little girl named Emily writes, "Dear God, Could you write more stories? We have already read all the ones you have and want to begin again!"[1] A lot of us have, indeed, read many of the stories in the Bible. If I asked a typical congregation for a show of hands on how many had read through the Bible from Genesis to Revelation, I have a feeling that not many hands would be lifted. Suppose I raised a second question to those who have read the Bible from Genesis to Revelation. Did you understand everything you read? Although the Bible is still popular and continues to be a national best seller, it is not authoritative for many because it is unread and not understood by most people.

A CLOSED BOOK TO MANY

People occasionally talk about the Bible or reflect on it in Sunday school or in a worship service, but many never read the Bible, which is supposed to be the church's chief source book. Although most homes in America have a Bible, it is a neglected book. How is the Bible used by most people who purchase it? It is filled with newspaper clippings of weddings or funerals; roses are pressed in it; and pictures of children, grandchildren, or other relatives are kept there. It lies on a table like a magic talisman, signifying that this family is religious.

The Bible is also considered by many people to be obsolete. They do not see how it relates in any way to the world in which they live today. "Why should I read it?" they ask. "There is nothing in the Bible that addresses modem science, medicine, computers, airplanes, television sets, or shopping malls." They ask bluntly, "What in the world can the Bible ever have to do with my life when it was written thousands of years ago?" The Bible to them is boring, dull, and totally unrelated to life where they live. It is even dull in its appearance with its dark black or blue cover and its narrow parallel columns and small print. Some say, "I've tried to read it, but it's impossible to understand, and I don't find it very interesting reading."

The Bible is also unfamiliar to many. "The Bible is," to use Bruce Barton's phrase, "the Book nobody knows." If I asked you to turn to the book of Hezekiah, I expect many of you might start searching for that book. But there is no such book in the Bible. It just sounds like it ought to be there. Many of us are like the young man who said, "I don't understand all this conversation about Dan and Beersheba. I thought they were husband and wife just like Sodom and Gomorrah." If you don't find that story humorous, it indicates something of the nature of the problem we have in studying the Bible. Most people are honestly not familiar with the contents of the Scriptures.

Linus was talking to Charlie Brown one day and observed: "I have begun to unfold the mysteries of the Bible." "Really!" Charlie Brown said. "How?" "I've started to read it!" Linus replied. The beginning place for knowledge of the Bible, of course, is to read the Bible. We can never understand the mystery of how people have sensed the pulse beat of God's presence through the written words if we never read the Bible.

THE BIBLE AS OUR SOURCE OF AUTHORITY

Authority is evident on many levels in our lives. There has to be some sense of authority or standard in education, for example, for us to determine if anyone has been properly educated. There has to be a standard in music or poetry against which poetry or music is judged. It jars the expectation when a writer does not follow normal poetical or musical customs. A writer or composer may move so far outside these boundaries that they produce only discord or chaos. Is there real music or poetry without some form of rhyme or notes? But is this not also true for medicine, law, sports, and the construction of houses, airplanes, cars, and other objects? In every life, there has to be some scale, guideline, polestar, system, or something that is the touchstone by which guidance is received. Every life reaches out for a sense of authority against which it measures itself.

Down through the centuries, the Bible has been the basis of authority for the church. The Bible has been the standard by which we as Baptists have measured our doctrines, polity, ministry, mission, practice, and behavior. The Bible has communicated the word of God to us. Throughout our heritage, we have declared boldly that the Scriptures have been our sole source of authority as Baptists.

THE SCRIPTURES DO NOT HAVE TO BE INERRANT

To declare that the Bible is our source of authority, however, does not mean the Scriptures must be infallible or inerrant. Infallibility and inerrancy are non-biblical terms. They are words to describe one narrow interpretation of Scripture. These words first entered the vocabulary of the church centuries ago when the Roman Catholic Church declared that when the pope spoke *ex cathedra*, his words were infallible and inerrant. It was only much later that certain religious leaders began to use such words to describe the Scriptures. Neither the biblical writers nor Jesus ever used such terms to talk about the Bible.

Advocates of inerrancy declare that the Bible cannot possibly contain any mistakes, inaccuracies, contradictions, or misstatements—not only in the realm of theology but of science, history, or any other area. "It is an absolutely perfect book without any error of any kind. A perfect God requires a perfect Bible," they assert. Those who commend an inerrancy view of Scripture quickly begin to put exceptions to or modifiers on their definition of inerrancy or infallibility. Some say, "Well, I mean not that the Bible we have today is inerrant but the original autographs—those early manuscripts that the original writers wrote." None of these are available today, of course, and no one has ever seen them and likely never will see them. It is a rather safe argument to declare that something one will never see is inerrant. If we did discover the autographs, however, I don't think we would find that the originals were inerrant either. If they were essential to our faith, why did

God not preserve them so we could have a perfect guide? Every translation is also an interpretation. Which translation is infallible?

Think with me about what kind of book the Bible really is. A good place to begin is by looking at some of the problems scholars and others have raised when they examined the Scriptures. Scholars have found from 150,000 to 250,000 variations in New Testament manuscripts alone![2] Sometimes those variations might be as simple as a misspelled word, an omitted word, a word that is repeated, a grammatical difference, or other mistakes made by a sleepy or careless scribe. Remember that all of the thousands of early manuscripts were written originally by hand and later copied by hand as they were passed on. None of these minute variations, however, makes the slightest difference in our understanding of the message about Christ, his ministry, and our redemption.

But do we not have to be honest about a problem like the quotation in Mark that is attributed to Isaiah when it is really from Malachi (Mark 1:2; Mal 3:1)? Matthew lists a quotation that he attributes to Jeremiah. Although the quotation cannot be located in Jeremiah, it does have a close parallel in Zechariah (Matt 27:9; Zech 11:12-13).

One also discovers that in 2 Samuel 10:18 the writer records that King David killed 700 Syrian chariot warriors, while in 1 Chronicles 19:18, where the same battle is described, the number killed by David is listed as 7,000. That discrepancy sounds like quite a ministerial exaggeration! How can both numbers be correct? This numerical difference does not change the real meaning of the story, but both numbers cannot be correct.

The inscription on the cross of Jesus is slightly different in all of the Gospels. Matthew, Mark, and Luke record that Jesus cleansed the temple at the end of his ministry, while John's Gospel states that the cleansing took place at the beginning of his ministry (Matt 21:12-13; Mark 11:15-17; Luke 18:4546; John 2:13-17). In Luke 24:4 and John 20:12, the authors note that two angels announced that Jesus was risen, while Matthew (28:2, 5) writes that it was only one.

In three of the Gospels, the roof through which the crippled man was lowered to the feet of Jesus was a typical Palestine roof made of mud and sticks. But in Luke's Gospel, the Gentile writer wrote that the roof was made of tile. In his Gentile country, that was the kind of roof with which he and his people were familiar (see Mark 2:4 and Luke 5:19).

If all Scripture is on the same level, what do we do with the passage that says Elisha the prophet, in the name of the Lord, cursed young children who called him bald-headed and then watched as bears came out of the woods and killed several of them (2 Kings 2:23-25)? That view is not on the same level with the statement of Jesus who said, "Love your enemies, do good to them who persecute you" (Luke 6:27).

THE BIBLE AS A RECORD OF REVELATION

Secondly, the Bible is authoritative for us because it is a record of God's revelation. Through the Scriptures we are able to see how God has dwelt with humanity down through the ages. Rather than falling out of heaven as a ready-made book, the Bible is a book that took thousands of years in development before it was collected together as we have it today. Sometimes a thousand years passed between the writing of one of the books and the writing of another. In the sixty-six books of the Bible, there are dozens of authors, not just one.

In a book like Genesis, scholars have demonstrated that there were a number of authors involved in the composition over a long period of time. Gradually, someone collected it as we have it today. That is why there are two creation stories, two flood stories, and two stories of this and two stories of that. The editor pulled the oral traditions together from various sources to form the book as we have it today.

The Bible was written by many different authors, with different perspectives, who were on different educational levels and who came from varied backgrounds. For a while, the material that later came to be called the Scriptures circulated orally among the people. Nothing was written down at all. This was true both in the formation of much of the Old Testament and the Gospels in the New Testament. The Bible did not come from the pen of one person but from the pen of dozens, and it took centuries to be formed as we know it today.

Within the Old Testament, references also appear to more than thirty other books from which Old Testament writers drew as sources. Many of these do not exist today. Historians are familiar with a few of these works, but most scholars have to admit they do not know the source of these extinct writings. The biblical writers quote directly from these nonextant books, and their quotations are included in our Scriptures. In what way were they inspired?

First and Second Kings were drawn from an ancient book called *The Annals of the Kings* of Israel (1 Kings 15:31; 2 Kings 13:8). This is not the same book as the biblical Chronicles, which was written long after *The Annals of the Kings*. The episode of Joshua causing the sun to stand still came from an ancient book of war songs called *The Book of the Just* or *The Book of Jasher* (Josh 10:13). "The Song of the Bow" by David, located in 2 Samuel 1:18, is also a fragment from this same book. These are the only records we have of the existence of this book. Numbers 21:14 refers to an old songbook called *The Wars of the Lord*, which is another ancient document that has perished. Scholars know nothing about the writers of these books or their origin. Yet our biblical writers quote them as their sources. The writer of the Gospel of Luke indicated that he was familiar with other writings about the life and ministry of Jesus (Luke 1:1-4).

The Bible developed over centuries from the pens of many different authors both in the Old Testament and the New Testament. Many of the biblical writers drew from a variety of sources as they gathered their material. The formation of the Scriptures was a long process. When you read the New Testament, you need to be aware that the books are not in the chronological order in which they were written. Paul's letters were written before the Gospels. The Gospel of John was likely the last Gospel written. The books were placed in the canon in the order we have them today to help readers sense the process of Israel's history and the coming of Christ and the beginning of the church.

What is the Bible? The Bible is a book filled with history, poetry, prophecy, biography, drama, parables, allegory, sermons, letters, and other types of writings to inspire us to learn to live better in the world. It has come to us from a great variety of backgrounds and places. No one is able say that he or she understands everything about its background or how it arrived in its present status. The Bible reveals a long developmental process in understanding God. People, as revealed within the Bible, were on many different levels when they responded to God's revelation.

One of the great mistakes in interpreting the Bible is to make the Bible a flat book. This view places everything in the Bible on the same level. Who honestly would want to put the statement in Psalm 137:9 (where the writer cries out in anger at the Babylonians, "Happy shall he be who takes your little ones and dashes them against the rock!") on the same level with the ones where Jesus says, "You are to love your enemies" (Matt 5:44) and "Turn the other cheek" (Matt 5:39)? If Scripture is inerrant, how does one explain the various levels of morality set forth in these passages? If all Scripture is verbally inspired, then the teachings in the Old Testament must be on the same level with those in the New Testament. This kind of flat view of the Bible presents difficult interpretation problems, to say the least.

Some people who put all Scripture on the same level have the bad practice of opening the Bible and selecting any verse their finger falls upon as the word of God for them. Did you hear about the man who used that method for his devotional reading? His finger fell on the passage where he read, "Judas went out and hanged himself." He flipped over and found another passage in the Bible and his finger fell on "Go thou and do likewise."

We cannot take all of the Bible literally. We have to understand the context, the situation, and the intent of the biblical writers. These are not the same in every situation. Paul reminded his readers in one of the Corinthian letters that our knowledge is fragmentary; we know in part and we see as though in a mirror, only a partial reflected truth (1 Cor 13:12).

THE BIBLE IS A DIVINE AND HUMAN BOOK

Thirdly, the Bible is both a divine and a human book. It is divine because it is inspired by God. Paul wrote to Timothy that "all Scripture is given by inspiration" (2 Tim 3:16). The word "inspired" means "God breathed." Technically Paul is writing about the Old Testament here. The Gospels had not been written, and Paul would never have dreamed that his letters would one day be a part of the church's canon.

God's presence has been revealed through the Scriptures. But remember God doesn't inspire books. God inspires people. The Bible is inspired because God first inspired people. God communicated his message to individuals, and they sat down and wrote. Some people would depict inspiration as though it were a mechanical transaction. This view seems to picture God overpowering a person by causing his or her hand to write the exact words he dictates. God speaks the words to the person and immediately the individual, robot-like, writes down what has been received. What kind of God would do that to people? Why would he choose to destroy their personalities? Would you want to worship a God who would so remove your personality from something you had written that you would not have any control over yourself in any way during this time? If this is the way God wrote the Bible, why did he need people at all? Why did he not write the books of the Bible with pen in his own hand rather than using the hand of another?

In Scriptures we read, "The word of the LORD came unto Jeremiah" or "The word of the LORD came unto Amos" or "The word of the LORD came unto Isaiah." God inspired people, not merely the books these people wrote. God's inspiration did not destroy their humanity. They were all human people with weaknesses and strengths, scholarly or unlettered, with ordinary or inferior gifts. For example, the language of the book of Hebrews is majestic, beautiful Greek. But the Greek of the book of Revelation is written as if by a child, an unlearned person, or a person for whom Greek was not his native tongue. The words seem like someone writing in a language that he doesn't know well. The Greek of the Gospel of Mark is on a sixth-grade level.

How do we explain the wide varieties of Greek if God inspired the writers? Simple! God let these people use their own knowledge and gifts to express themselves. Sometimes Paul wrote in long, dangling sentences that would not pass freshman English. But remember that Paul dictated his letters to a friend most of the time. Sometimes he left the verb out or forgot what his subject was. That is one of the reasons it is often so difficult to understand some of Paul's letters.

God worked through human instruments to convey his message. God has never asked that his servants be perfect. After all, he chose Abraham, Jacob, Moses, Simon Peter, Thomas, and many others to be his instruments. They were all frail human beings, just as we are.

Everywhere you touch the Bible, it reverberates with life. It sobs and sings with the pain of Job, the rejection of Jeremiah, the hope of Isaiah, the frustration of Jonah, the sin of David, the hatred of a psalmist, the security of another psalmist, the courage of Queen Esther, the challenge of Amos, the doubt of Thomas, the promise of John, the faith of Paul, the failure and forgiveness of Peter, the grace of God, and the hope of eternal life.

One of the first heresies in the early church was called Gnosticism. Gnosticism denied the humanity of Jesus. Gnostics believed that Jesus was divine, the Son of God, but they denied that he was human in any way. The Gospel of John and several other New Testament writings were written to refute that heresy. The Gospel of John affirmed that "the word became flesh and dwelt among us" (1:14). Jesus' humanity was essential for the incarnation to be real. The humanity of the Bible must also be affirmed. To deny the humanity of the Scriptures is heresy. Heresy is not rejecting inerrancy. Heresy is rejecting the humanity of the biblical writers. This heresy is similar to that of the Gnostics because it sees only the divine nature of the Bible. To deny the humanity of the biblical writers makes them appear like robots for

God and destroys their personalities. The Bible is divine because God inspired the human writers, but the Bible is also human because God worked through normal, imperfect people.

If I were dying of thirst in a desert and someone came along and offered me a cup of water to ease my thirst, I wouldn't look over and say, "Wait a minute. Before I can drink from this cup I have to see if it has been properly sterilized. Is the cup bone china or tin? Does the cup have any cracks, chips, or dents in it? Is that distilled water?" That would be foolishness! I would drink the water because I am dying of thirst. The water meets my needs. What the container is like is not that important. It does not have to be perfect.

What a marvelous book the Bible is! It is both a human and divine book. It is human because God worked through ordinary people to bring it into existence. He worked through their gifts and personalities to convey his message. It is divine because it is the record of God's relationship to humanity. It conveys God's message to us today. It continues to provide us a guide for living and understanding God and Jesus.

THE BIBLE AS AUTHORITATIVE FOR FAITH AND PRACTICE

Fourthly, the Bible is authoritative for faith and practice. This has been the basic position of Baptists since our beginning. It is authoritative for us in matters of faith—how we understand God, Christ, the Holy Spirit, and the church—and in the way we practice how we live and minister in our Christian life. The Bible is not a book of science, medicine, or engineering. In these areas we do not seek to make it authoritative. But it is authoritative in matters of faith and practice.

A primitive view of the universe is found in the Old Testament. The writers describe a flat earth with four corners. The heavens are depicted as an upturned bowl resting on pillars. Rain comes from a sea above the heavens and is let in through the "windows of heaven."[3] People everywhere believed these primitive notions at that time. The Bible was written in a prescientific age and was never intended to be a book of science for the twenty-first century.

Have you ever seen the play or the movie titled *Inherit the Wind?* It is based on the Scopes trial where Clarence Darrow, the famous attorney, debated with the pious and political William Jennings Bryan. Darrow was defending a science teacher who was on trial for teaching evolution. He had brought a rock to his science class and said it was millions of years old. William Jennings Bryan said there was no way this could be possible because the world was only six thousand years old. He based his belief on the teaching of Bishop James Usher, who said the creation took place exactly in 4004 BC on October 23 at 9 A.M. The courtroom broke into laughter when Darrow asked sarcastically, "Was that Eastern Standard Time? It wasn't Daylight Saving Time, was it? Because the Lord didn't make the sun until the fourth day."[4]

Even if you take Genesis literally, the days that are mentioned cannot be twenty-four-hour periods as we know them because the sun was not created until the fourth day. We back ourselves into a ridiculous corner when we try to press science under the authority of the Bible. Bishop Usher was a noted scholar in his day, but he was wrong. The world is not just six thousand years old. It is millions of years old. The purpose of the Bible is religion, not science. The point of Genesis is to inform its readers that God is Creator. It tells us who, not how. God is the Creator. Science can help us understand how the world was created, but not by whom or why.

CHRIST IS LORD OF THE SCRIPTURES

Fifthly, Jesus Christ is Lord of the Scriptures. The Scriptures are measured by Jesus Christ. Christ is Lord of the Scriptures as well as of our life. Jesus said to the scribes and Pharisees, "You diligently search the Scriptures because you think they give you eternal life" (John 5:39). Hillel, a rabbinic sage and Jewish scholar (c. 60 BC–AD 30), observed, "If a man has gained for himself the words of the law, he has gained for himself life in the world to come."[5] These religious leaders actually believed that diligent study of the Scriptures earned eternal life. They assumed that "life" was in the Scriptures, the written word. But Jesus said, "It is they [the Scriptures] that bear witness of me" (John 5:40). We get our focus all twisted around when we end within the Scriptures themselves and do not see that their purpose is to point us to God.

Jesus obviously loved the Old Testament. He quoted from it often. But Jesus never used the word "inerrancy" or spoke about inspiration. Notice that Jesus clearly stated that he had superseded the ancient Scriptures. When he declared, "It has been said unto you . . . but now I say unto you" (Matt 5:39), he made one of the most radical challenges ever made to the ancient Jewish law. Notice what Jesus has said preceding this, which some people often quote to prove that he did not intend to change the Old Testament Scriptures. Jesus said, "I have come not to destroy the law and the prophets but to fulfill them" (Matt 5:17). He has come to "fulfill" them. What does that mean? To fulfill means that he accomplished the original intention of the law and the prophets. He came to complete their purpose in leading people to God and living out God's will in the world. Laws were meant to serve people, not bind them in inflexible chains of customs and traditions.

The words "but I say unto you" are remarkable. Jesus Christ had come to present a new Mt. Sinai. His words marked a great divide between the old way and the new. "It has been said unto you, but now I say unto you" is used six times in this passage from Matthew. Jesus contradicts, refutes, changes, reinterprets, transforms, alters, and even rejects some of the Old Testament laws and traditions and points to a higher, deeper insight into the meaning of the law and the prophets as he directs his followers to understand more meaningful ways of following God.

Jesus came to conserve the real meaning of the law and the prophets and not the oral traditions and rituals that the scribes and Pharisees had established. He probed beneath ceremonial and written regulations to the ethical principles behind these teachings. Our Lord broke through the rigid restrictions of the law, which bound people to the literalism of the text, to the deeper meaning behind the words. Jesus constantly distinguished between the significant and the superfluous in Old Testament teachings. He spoke out against their rigid dogmatism and declared that their approach had suppressed truth. He charged, "So, for the sake of your tradition, you have made void the word of God" (Matt 15:6).

The word *authority* and the word *author* both come from the same Latin root that means to create or produce. The authority of Christ is not by coercion, power, force, or manipulation, but by love. Jesus said, "And I, if I be lifted up, I will draw all men unto me" (John 12:32). His authority attracts people to the grace of God.

Jesus Christ is the standard by which we judge the level of the Scriptures. He is Lord of the Scriptures. The writer of the book of Hebrews stated that truth in these words: "When in former times God spoke to our forefathers, he spoke in fragmentary and various fashion through the prophets. But in this the final age he has spoken to us in the Son" (Heb 1:1-2). John tells us that the whole purpose of his Gospel was "that you might believe that Jesus is the Christ, the Son of God and that believing you might have life in his name" (John 20:31). Jesus is Lord of the Scriptures.

Therefore, if passages in the Old Testament depict a view of God that is sub-Christian or show a low view of morality, we are not bound by these teachings. We are not bound by the ancient ceremonial laws or the ancient priestly traditions of the Old Testament. Our standard is Jesus Christ. He has revealed the nature of God to us.

My wife occasionally goes away for a few days on a trip to Kentucky and North Carolina. Suppose I got a letter from her. That would be nice. I could sit down, read it, and enjoy it. What would you think if I enjoyed reading the letter so much that I began to underline the verbs and subjects in it and analyzed it line by line? Suppose when Emily came home, I ignored her and continued to read her letter. I might come up to you and say, "I want to show you this letter that I got from Emily. It is the most wonderful letter. It keeps me informed about what she is doing. It means so much to me." But someone might say, "I thought Emily came home." "Yes, she did," I would say. "But look at this letter I got from her." If I continued to ignore Emily and only read the letter, you would know something was wrong with me, wouldn't you?

The Bible is to direct us to God. It is not an end in itself. When we make the Bible an end in itself and seek to make it inerrant and infallible, that becomes bibliolatry—the worship of a book.

God has spoken to us through the Scriptures. The Scriptures tell us of God's love and grace. But as Luther says, "The Scriptures are the cradle that contains the Christ." The Scriptures point us to God. They are not God. We are not to confuse the lover and the letters. "In the beginning was the Word and the Word was with God and the Word was God . . . . And the Word became flesh and dwelt among us" (John 1:1, 14). The Word did not become more words. The Word of God did not become ideas. The Word of God became flesh—a human person. The Word became incarnate. We worship the God who has revealed himself through Jesus Christ as a living Lord. The God of the Bible is a Lord who has always revealed himself in events, especially in the Exodus, and supremely in Jesus.

THE BIBLE CONTINUES TO SPEAK

Then, finally, the Bible is authoritative because it is a living Word. Although the Bible was written in the past, it must not be confined to the past. God's Spirit continues to speak through the Bible today. That is the reason you and I are Christians today. God did not say everything he intended to say in the past and then quit talking. The Bible has continued to reveal God's word through the ages. It can speak to you and me today because God's Spirit continues to communicate to your needs and mine. I read the Bible, but I am also read by it. I read its words, but the words enable me to sense *the* Word, the Eternal God.

In the second letter to Timothy (2 Tim 3:15-17), Paul tells us so clearly how this happens. Timothy, from his youth up, had been nurtured in the Scriptures by his mother and grandmother. We learn wisdom that leads to salvation through the Scriptures. The Scriptures reveal the redemptive grace of God and how men and women might experience this salvation. The Scriptures point us to Christ. The story about the Ethiopian eunuch in Acts 8:26-40 reveals how Philip interpreted the Scriptures, which led to the man's conversion. The Scriptures seek to lead us to salvation. The Bible is not our salvation. It leads us *to* salvation.

The Scriptures are also for the purpose of teaching, instructing, and guiding us deeper into the faith. Jesus is the Master Teacher, and he has called us to be disciples—learners.

Sometimes our seminary professors receive a lot of criticism from those who do not understand the purpose of seminary teaching. One of my New Testament professors at Southeastern Baptist Theological Seminary was R. C. Briggs. Dr. Briggs told about an experience he had when he was a pastor. There was a lot of opposition to and criticism of the Revised Standard Version of the Bible, which had just been published. At the Wednesday night prayer meeting of the church where he was then pastor, Dr. Briggs took enough copies of the Greek New Testament to pass among his church members. After he distributed the Greek testaments, he asked, "Brother Jones, would you now read to us from the first chapter of the Gospel of John." "But . . . but I can't do that," the man said. "I can't read Greek." "Oh, you can't read Greek. So somebody has to translate it for you," Dr. Briggs responded. "Well, since you can't read Greek, you will have to accept somebody's translation. Are you going to believe some Anglican in the sixteenth century or would you rather believe some modern person in the twentieth-century, like evangelicals, which include some Baptists?" He said that about two dozen people placed orders for the Revised Standard Version that night.

Somebody had to translate the Bible from the Hebrew and Greek, or none of us could read it. Thank God for our dedicated scholars who have devoted themselves to knowing how to read and interpret the Scriptures! We, like Timothy, are continually taught and nurtured by them.

Paul continues by saying that the Scriptures are also for rebuke and correction. The Scriptures often convict us of our sin and point us to God. When you read the Scriptures, remember most of all that they need to read you. The Word of God comes into your life and judges you. It lifts a mirror in front of you. It brings God's Spirit before us to address our lives and show us how far removed we are from God's way, the goal to which he has beckoned us and the kind of life he wants us to live. Look at the mirror in the Bible that is lifted up for us to see our image. As Søren Kierkegaard has said, the Scriptures are "a letter from God with your personal address on it." See your name written in the Bible. God is speaking to you through the Bible. The assurance of the writer of the Twenty-third Psalm becomes a word of encouragement to you. The doubt of Thomas reflects your own struggle with faith. The denial of Peter reminds you of your own weakness. The disciples' request of Jesus to teach them how to pray becomes your own plea. The Bible is a timeless book. It speaks to you today out of the life of a people from the past.

The Scriptures, Paul says, call us to righteous living so that we can be equipped to live for God (for every good work). The Scriptures are not intended just for our reading; we are supposed to understand their message so we can take that message into the world. All of our reading needs to be translated into service and ministry for him.

Have you ever been in some giant cathedral and seen a sign near a Bible that was chained to the pulpit? In one such church, the sign read, "This book is not to be taken from this building." Unfortunately, there are a lot of people who have that notion about the Bible. You are not supposed to take the Bible outside the church; it has to remain within the walls of the church. The Scriptures are not an end in themselves but a vehicle, an instrument, to enable us to live more fully the Christlike life.

Suppose you and I are lost in a mountain wilderness. We have no food and we know that snow will be coming soon. We stumble into a cabin. While we are sitting there wondering what to do, we notice a faded old map lying on the table. It is torn and has holes in it. It is dirty and part of it seems to be missing. It is an imperfect instrument in every way imaginable. But you and I look at it and note that there is a line drawn on this map that shows a path leading from the cabin down the mountain to a main road below where we could find help. You ask, "I wonder if this can be true. Can this map be correct? Will it lead us to safety? Will it save us?" We will not know until we follow the map. Well, as we follow the map down the mountainside, we discover that it does indeed bring us to safety and help. We know the map is trustworthy because we have followed it. Whether it is marred, faded, or has holes in it, or whether it is dirty, long, short, new, old, green, blue, or whatever, we know it is true and reliable because it has led you and me and others to safety.

The Bible has been that kind of map for many people for centuries. It does not have to be a perfect map to guide us in our spiritual pilgrimage. Elizabeth Achtemeier, the late noted biblical scholar, observed, "The Bible was not arbitrarily chosen by the early church as some fixed and eternal rule. The Bible became the authority for the church because the church learned, over decades of worship and practice, that the biblical story was the one story that created and sustained its life."[6]

I love the Bible. I have devoted my life to studying it and seeking to understand it and communicate its message to others. The Bible has withstood kings, popes, agnostics, atheists, various interpretations—including heresy, translations, mistranslations, and controversy. It has withstood rejection, abandonment, desertion, liberalism, modernism, fundamentalism, hatred, evil, ridicule, and even preaching! But for people, the Bible is a cup of fresh water for a thirsty spirit. The Bible is rain on parched soil. It is comfort for an aching heart. It is bread for a hungry soul. It has provided directions down the path of life. It offers help through the valley of the shadow of death. It is light on the darkest of days. It is guidance in defeat and despair. It is a word among words. It is a song in the night. It is life to the dead. It gives us the pulsebeat of God, the embrace of God's presence. Its words guide us *to* the Word.

NOTES

[1] Eric Marshall and Stuart Hample, comps., *Children's Letters to God* (New York: Essandess Special Edition, 1967).

[2] M. M. Parvis, "New Testament Text," *The Interpreter's Dictionary of the Bible, R-Z*, ed. George Buttrick (New York: Abingdon Press, 1962), 595.

[3] See Gen 1:6-8; 7:11; Job 37:8; 26:11; Pss 104:4; 148:4; and Isa 40:22.

[4] Jerome Lawrence and Robert E. Lee, *Inherit the Wind* (New York: Random House, 1955).

[5] Quoted in George R. Beasley-Murray, *John*, Word Biblical Commentary 36 (Waco: Word Books, 1987), 78.

[6] Elizabeth Achtemeier, *Creative Preaching: Finding the Words* (Nashville: Abingdon Press, 1980), 19.

CHAPTER FOUR

The Autonomy and Vitality of the Local Church

Several years ago I read about two men who lived on a houseboat. They had it securely tied up at a waterfront dock. One night while they were sleeping, a bad storm rose and the boat broke its moorings and drifted out to sea. The next morning one of them woke up and, looking outside, ran back and yelled to his friend, "Wake up! Wake up! We are not here anymore!"

There are a lot of people who are saying that the church is not the same anymore. They believe the church has drifted down the rivers and lakes of life in a direction that is radically different from what our Lord intended for it to be. Some voices declare that the church is always dying. But other voices note rather quickly, "Yes, but it never does." A woman once said that she did not think the church was any longer related to the first century nor did it have anything to say to the age in which she was living. This indictment against the church says that the church is both unbiblical and irrelevant.

But many have united themselves with the church, and some, like I, have identified with a particular Baptist church, believing the church is still meaningful. In a few pages I want to see if we can sense, capture, or recapture something of the emphasis that Baptists have tried to place on the church. Within a brief compass no one can do justice to the great theme of the church. But let's explore its meaning.

Paul Minear, the New Testament scholar, has said that there are at least ninety-six different images of the church in the New Testament.[1] The images range from simple words like believers, disciples, faithful, and saints to the shrine of the Eternal, the bride of Christ, the new Israel, the new humanity, salt, light, leaven, and many others. Rather than having just one picture of the church, the New Testament presents a picture gallery of images. The word "church" appears in the Gospels only in Matthew 16:18 and 18:17, and these passages have been a storm center of debate. The Greek word for church, *ekklesia*, literally means "the called out."

THE UNIVERSAL CHURCH

As Baptists, we believe strongly in the local church, but we must be aware that the New Testament also speaks about a universal church. This image of the church reaches beyond any local setting of a particular church. Dale Moody, in his commentary on Ephesians, observes that our contemporary society has, what he calls, an edifice complex.[2] Many identify the church with its buildings. For the first 300 years of its existence, the church had no buildings. Christians met in catacombs, houses, or converted synagogues. Today people have a tendency to think that the building is the church. We even teach our children a saying that we symbolize with our fingers and hands: "Here's the church, there's the steeple, open the door and there's the people!" Ah! But that is not right! The church is the people, not the building! The church cannot be identified with its structure.

Paul uses a number of images about the church in Ephesians. In the second chapter of Ephesians he moves from depicting the church as a body, to the church as a commonwealth, to the figure in the second chapter of the church as a building or temple. But Paul was not restricting the church to a particular building. In other places Paul writes about the church as the body of Christ (Eph 5) and the bride of Christ (Eph 1 and 2). Jesus said, "I will build *my* church" (Matt 18:18). The church our Lord is continuing to build cannot be confined to buildings. W. O. Carver, one of our noted Baptist New Testament scholars, wrote, "In view of the biblical figure of the church as Christ's bride, the insistence of some that all uses of the term 'church' in the New Testament refer only to local organizations becomes absurd almost to the point of sacrilege, attributing to Christ a bride in every locality where a church is found."[3] There is a wider dimension to the church than any local setting can ever express. The New Testament gives a heavenly vision, or an ideal depiction, of the church our Lord founded.

The church, of course, is not equated with the kingdom of God. But the biblical view of the church extends far beyond every local dimension of this universal image. Southern Baptists acknowledged this perspective in their revision of *The Baptist Faith and Message*, article 6, in 1963. After a discussion of the church as "a local body of baptized believers," the following sentence was added: "The New Testament speaks also of the church as the body of Christ which includes all of the redeemed of all the ages." This statement was not removed from the 2000 version of the *Baptist Faith and Message*. In Hebrews 12:1 the writer refers to "a great cloud of witnesses" that continue to surround the saints today. The church can never be limited to a local setting. There is the church Jesus founded and local churches are expressions of that universal church.

THE CHURCH AS LOCAL

But the church as we know it best is the not-so-holy local congregation. As members of a local congregation, we are also the church. We are a part of the church. There is "the scandal of particularity." The church does have a place, and we are a part of the church in some particular place. Sometimes it is easy to believe in ideals but harder to express them in a concrete way. It is easy to talk about being patriotic. But it is much more difficult to be willing to serve your country or to sacrifice your life for your country. It is easy to talk about the ideals of motherhood or fatherhood, but it is much more difficult to be a good mother or a good father at home. We can talk about justice as a theory, but it becomes much more difficult when we have to treat someone justly with whom we radically differ or who has committed some awful crime. It is easy to talk about brotherhood and sisterhood, but it is much harder to treat people of another race or culture as equals or to end apartheid or racial injustice wherever it occurs.

Do you see the difference? It is easy to talk about the church as an ideal. But the church we know best is the one in local settings where we live every day. In the New Testament, Paul's letters were written "to the saints who are in Ephesus" (Eph 1:1), "to the church of God that is in Corinth" (1 Cor 1:2), "to all God's beloved in Rome" (Rom 1:7), "to all the saints in Jesus

Christ who are in Philippi" (Phil 1:1), and "to the church of the Thessalonians" (1 Thess 1:1). Paul's letters were written to local churches as he attempted to address particular needs they had.

Carver has reminded us of the local nature of the church in these lines: "The church is the core of God's Kingdom as realized in human history. Local churches are the agencies of that kingdom and of its gospel; they are 'colonies' of the kingdom on earth, located in the midst of the world which is to be won through the gospel."[4] Each local church is a particular expression—a colony, if you please—of Christ's church in the world. As members of a local congregation, we bear witness to Christ where we live in this particular moment of human history.

I received a telephone call one night from a man who wanted to attend the worship service when I was pastor at St. Matthews Baptist Church. "Where is your church?" he asked. I knew what he was asking. He wanted the location of our church building, a street address. But I wanted to tell him that our church gathered on Sunday at 3515 Grandview Avenue to worship and then scattered throughout the week to serve the God we worshiped on Sunday. "Where is your church?" The answer to that question depends on whether one thinks of the church as being gathered or scattered, doesn't it?

CHRIST IS THE HEAD OF THE CHURCH

Go further with me and remember that, although the church may be local, it is under the Lordship of Christ. This is one of the central emphases throughout Ephesians and many of Paul's other epistles. Jesus Christ is the head of the church. "And God has put all things under his feet and has made him head over all things for the church" (Eph 1:22). Paul uses another metaphor in Ephesians 2:20 of Christ as the chief cornerstone. Some scholars believe this stone was a huge seven-foot foundation stone. Others are convinced that this stone was the gemstone placed in the archway that held the whole structure together. Whatever stone it was, the gemstone or the foundation stone, it was the keystone on which the whole structure depended. Jesus Christ is this stone. He is Lord of the church.

In one sense, then, we can speak of our local church as being our own. But in a higher sense, it is the Lord's church. The church and all local expressions of the universal church are under his authority. It is Christ who owns and governs the church, and we seek to serve Jesus Christ as the Lord of the church. The "Abstract of Principles" of the Southern Baptist Theological

Seminary, article XIV, written in 1858, contains these lines: "The Lord Jesus is the Head of the church, which is composed of all his true disciples and in Him is invested supremely all power for its government."[5] Our local churches always serve under the authority of Christ. We govern ourselves, but we need to remember that the will of Christ is not always determined by a majority vote. A majority may express their prejudices or selfish ends. As "members of the household of God" (Eph 2:19), we are under the ultimate authority of God.

It has always been interesting to me to notice that some churches refuse to put a cross on their steeple, but they will put weathervanes there instead. What does that symbol mean? Does the symbol of the weathervane mean that a church makes its decision on the basis of which way the wind is blowing? Unfortunately too many churches make their decisions that way. Public opinion dictates the direction those churches take. Whether the issue under discussion in a local church concerns attitudes toward racial minorities, ecology, war and peace, world hunger, homelessness, or other matters, it should be decided under a sense of the Lordship of Christ and not merely by a majority vote. Our churches are local, but they exist under Christ as Lord.

RECONCILED BELIEVERS

The local congregation is also supposed to be composed of reconciled believers. These regenerate believers are individuals who have committed their lives to Christ as Lord. The church is not simply a sweet social gathering where people come together to feel better. The church is supposed to contain individuals who acknowledge Jesus Christ as Lord of their lives. The ministry of the church is derived from and dependent upon its Lord.

One of the clear thrusts of our Lord's ministry is that it is a ministry of reconciliation. Jesus said, "I have come to seek and to save that which is lost" (Luke 19:10). Our world is filled with all kinds of lostness and brokenness. Men and women are estranged from God. They are fragmented in their relationships with one another and do not understand their authentic personhood. Jesus told various parables to describe different ways individuals could be lost. He told a parable about a lost sheep that wandered off from the rest of the flock. Sometimes the lostness we experience can be aimlessness, purposelessness, meaninglessness—life without direction or guidance. Many are busy going without knowing where they are going.

Some of us are lost as in the parable about the woman who drops coins and diligently sweeps the floor until she finds the coins. Like the good shepherd, this woman "seeks the coins until she finds them." This lostness is not the result of personal choice. Some people are victims of circumstances, and whatever has happened to create their lostness is not really their fault. Environmental factors have created their situations and they are simply caught in the web of life. They have been influenced by their friends, schoolmates, families, and others. They were caught by these circumstances and pulled down the paths of sin.

Others are lost like the Prodigal Son whom Jesus described in a parable. Our lostness is our own making. We set our own direction. We have rebelled. We have wasted our goods, our way, and have turned away from the Father and gone to a far country to waste our life in riotous living. Still others, though, have a lostness like the elder brother. But they are still lost. They are lost in self-righteousness and respectability. They see themselves as superior to other people and remain unaware that they are still lost, cut off, and fragmented from God.

Three times in Paul's Second Epistle to the Corinthian church (5:18-28) he writes about men and women being reconciled to God. It was not God who needed to be reconciled to us. We are the ones who needed to repent and surrender to his love. Sin had not made God stop loving us. The root idea of the word "reconciliation" is change. Reconciliation is a changed relationship. A relationship with God that was broken and fragmented has been restored. Reconciliation has provided us with a new relationship with God.

Without apology the church proclaims that all people are sinners in need of God's mercy and are reconciled to God by grace. This is one of the foundational teachings of the church. As an evangelistic people, we gladly proclaim the good news of Christ to others.

At the founding of the Baptist World Alliance on July 17, 1905, in London, England, one of the noted preachers for that historic meeting was J. D. Freeman, pastor of Bloor Street Baptist Church in Toronto, Canada. He began by stressing the essential Baptist principle of the sovereignty of Christ, which he characterized as "the master-fact of religious experiences." Freeman continued in these descriptive words:

> It is the nerve centre of our denominational sensibility. It is the
> spinal column of our theology. It is the bed-rock of our church
> polity. It is the mainspring of our missionary activity. It is the

sheet-anchor of our hope. It is the crown of our rejoicing. For to this end Christ both died and lived again, that He might be Lord both of the dead and the living. From this germinant conception all our distinctive denominational principles emerge. As the oak springs from the acorn, so our many-branched Baptist life is developed from this seed of thought. Baptistic Christianity lives and moves and has its being in the realm of the doctrine of the sovereignty of Christ.

In the terms of this conception we express our root idea of Christianity. In its last analysis Christianity means to us the union of a human life with Jesus Christ; this union, involving on the one hand a relation of personal saviourhood and sovereignty, and on the other a relation of personal trust and love and loyalty. This is Christianity stated in terms of its irreducible minimum.[6]

Christ is our Lord. Our churches are based on the confession of Christ as Lord. It is the central basis of who we are as the people of Christ. We declare that fact without apology. The invitation to experience God's reconciliation is extended to young and old, the educated and uneducated, male and female, rich and poor, black and white—to all people.

Our churches sometimes become so intent on growing, on building numbers, that the threshold of the entrance to the church becomes so low that people, who become church members, are not confronted with the radical call to commit their life to Christ as Lord. They simply join the church. J. D. Smart cautions the church that the "emphasis upon growth leads easily to a lowering of standards, so that people are swept into the membership of the church without any adequate preparation for it, without any clear confrontation with the claims of the gospel and so without any real decision of faith." He continues further by noting that: "The apology for this procedure is sometimes made that now at least they are within the circle of the church and the church has the opportunity of reaching them with its gospel. But when they find so many already inside the church who know little more of what it all means than they do, are they likely to take seriously their need for anything more?"[7]

Our basic foundational principle is a call for every church member to acknowledge Jesus Christ as Lord. To fail at this point is to undercut the experience essential for church membership.

BELIEVER'S BAPTISM

When a person has made a confession of faith, he or she is baptized by immersion. When the disciples of Jesus were first called Christians in Antioch, "baptism" was a term their enemies used against them. The word "Baptist" was first used in ridicule against our forefathers. Now both of these words, Christians and Baptists, which were first used in ridicule and disdain, have become titles of honor. As Baptists, we baptize only believers by immersion. Baptism takes place after a person has confessed Jesus Christ as Lord.

One's commitment to God must be conscious, necessarily free, and voluntary. An inner experience with God cannot be compelled nor can a commitment be made for someone else. H. Wheeler Robinson, a Baptist scholar and former principal of Regent's Park College at Oxford, has stated the Baptist position well on the reason for "believers" baptism that is administered on a profession of personal faith in Christ:

> The common element in all these interpretations of baptism is the necessary *passivity* of the infant baptized. Whether baptism be called dedication, or covenanting by parents, or the sealing of a divine covenant, or an actual regeneration, it is throughout something done to, nothing done by, the baptized. So far as he is concerned, all of them are non-moral acts, though the act of the parents or sponsors is properly moral. The Baptist position is not simply a new phase of this succession of interpretations; it stands outside of them all as *the only baptism which is strictly and primarily an ethical act on the part of the baptized.*[8]

Baptism, like conversion, is not a passive act. Somebody else cannot "experience" it for another person. No one else can have faith for me or for you. Each of us must make a decision about baptism for himself or herself. George Beasley-Murray, in his scholarly book, *Baptism In the New Testament,* draws this conclusion:

> Against every tendency of New Testament theologians to mini-
> mize the Pauline doctrine of faith, it must be insisted that in his
> teaching, faith in God manifested in Christ is *prior* to baptism
> and faith receives the gift of God *in* baptism, and faith in God is
> the constitutive principle of the Christian life *after* baptism.
> There is not a line in Paul's writing that justifies a reversal of this
> emphasis in the relationship between the two.[9]

As Baptists, we believe in baptizing those who make a profession of faith in Christ. Baptism is, as H. Wheeler Robinson says, "an acted parable."[10] In his letter to the Romans, Paul gives a vivid description of what happens when we are baptized with Christ. "What are we to say, then?" Paul wrote. "Shall we persist in sin, so that there may be all the more grace? No, no! We die to sin; how can we live in it any longer? Have you forgotten that when we were baptized into union with Christ Jesus we were baptized into his death? By baptism we were buried with him, and lay dead, in order that, as Christ was raised from the dead in the splendour of the Father, so also we might set our feet upon the new path of life" (Rom 6:1-4, NEB).

In our baptism we are identified with Christ. Baptism is a confessional sign, symbol, statement, and experience about our dying to the old way of a life of sin and now being identified with Christ's death so that we might be raised to walk in newness of life through the power of his resurrection. As Paul writes in another place, "I am crucified with Christ, nevertheless, I live, yet not I but Christ lives in me" (Gal 2:20). We believe that the most authentic way to signify this radical experience is through baptism by immersion. Immersion is the most expressive way of showing the believer's identification with Christ and his way of life. As conversion is a life-changing experience, baptism by immersion is a drastic experience for the believer in his or her identification with Christ's experience of death and resurrection.

THE AUTONOMY OF THE LOCAL CHURCH

We believe in the autonomy of the local church. This means that each congregation has self-rule or self-government. No group outside our congregation can dictate to us how to run the church where I am pastor. This belief is one of the bedrocks of our tradition. No other religious, ecclesiastical, or convention body can tell us how to conduct our business.

Theron Rankin, one of the former secretaries of the Foreign Mission Board of the Southern Baptist Convention, once wrote:

> The most pronounced belief and practice of Baptists, as I have known them in the South, is the sovereignty of each local church, and the conviction that no Convention has biblical authority to determine the practice of individual churches . . . . As someone has recently said, "the convention cannot be an organization or an agency that tells churches what they can or cannot do." The churches tell the Convention what it can do.[11]

Each church seeks to govern itself. We begin in our churches with the awareness that an individual who commits his or her life to Christ, does so because that individual has direct access to God. We do not have to go through some priest or some ecclesiastical, governmental agency to reach God. This means each congregation determines its own government, worship, organizations, and programs. Each local church recognizes no hierarchy beyond itself. (This will be expounded more in the discussion on the priesthood of believers in the next chapter.)

All Christians are on an equal level in our churches. Every member has a right to voice his or her opinions in the government of our church. We may have a variety of gifts, but all are seen as priests before God. We can speak about Baptist churches but never *the* Baptist church.

In *The Second London Confession*, dated 1677, our Baptist pioneers wrote, "To each of these churches gathered, according to Christ's mind, declared in his Word, he hath given all that power and authority, which is any way needful, for their carrying out that order in worship, and discipline, which he hath instituted them to observe."[12] Here again is the acknowledgment that Christ is the ultimate authority for the church—the head of the church—but the local church has the authority to carry out the work and ministry of his church in the world.

Dr. Barrie White, a Baptist historian and principal for several years at Regents Park College at Oxford, England, was asked one time what the seventeenth-century Baptists were like. He observed that seventeenth-century Baptists would usually gather together in the house of one of the believers or in a small church building. About twenty or thirty would be present. They would form a circle. Each one would open the Bible and all would take turns reading a passage and commenting upon it. There was no single preacher for the service. No one person ever presented the only way the others could interpret the Bible. That approach continues to be seen in our Sunday schools today. The Baptist preacher does not speak for or have the only interpretation in a local congregation. It has always been our Baptist polity that each church and each individual has the right and freedom to interpret the Scriptures.

THE COOPERATIVE ALLIANCE WITH OTHER CHURCHES

At the same time that Baptists affirm the autonomy of the local church, the freedom of self-rule for each congregation, we also have joined in a cooperative way with other Baptists and fellow Christians. This action has always been a voluntary response of each congregation. Neither the district association, state convention, national convention, nor the Baptist World Alliance has any authority over the local congregation. We participate in all of these organizations on a voluntary basis. Someplace in the introduction to all of these groups is a statement that none of these bodies is legislative or judicial. Christ is always declared the sole authority for the church. These groups are utilized in an advisory or administrative way. As H. Wheeler Robinson observed:

> No one can understand the life of the denomination who does not realize that all larger groupings of Baptist Churches are for common action by representatives, not for the exercise of authoritative control. The local Churches join or withdraw from these as they see fit, though in practice there is stable union and a large measure of joint activity.[13]

These groups should not attempt to exercise control over the churches that engage together in a cooperative way. Each church's participation is voluntary and indicates a desire to expand its ministry by working with others. Each draws support, comfort, and strength from one another.

One of the first Baptist associations known to us is the one formed in Abingdon, England, in October 1652. They indicated the importance of cooperation in these words: "There is the same relation betwixt the perticular [sic] churches each towards others as there is betwixt perticular members of one church . . . and they ought to manifest its care over other churches as fellow members of the same body of Christ."

They acknowledged that no Christian should try to live out his or her faith in isolation. So each church needed the strength and support it drew from other Baptist churches as they worked in a cooperative way. This cooperation, they said, would help them bear each other's burdens and rejoice at one another's victories. Cooperation would give them counsel in difficult matters and prevent prejudices against each other. These and other reasons led them to conclude "that perticular churches in Christ ought to hold a firme communion each with other."[14]

This binding with other Baptist churches did not undermine the local Baptist church. They were always seen as free and distinctive. This is a hallmark of our beliefs. Neither the local Baptist association, the state Baptist convention, the Southern Baptist Convention, the American Baptist Convention, the Cooperative Baptist Fellowship, or the Baptist World Alliance can tell any church what they must think, believe, or practice as a Baptist church. On a voluntary basis, we participate, support, and join these organizations, and we can withdraw from any of them if we so choose. This was clearly stated in the London Confession of Faith in 1644:

> That being thus joyned, every Church has power given them from Christ for their better well-being, to choose to themselves meet persons into the office of Pastors, Teachers, Elders, Deacons, being qualified according to the Word . . . and that none other have power to impose them, either these or any other.[15]

THE PRIMACY OF WORSHIP

Baptists also see the local congregation as the center for worship. We acknowledge that worship is primary. In Paul's metaphor of the building in Ephesians, he notes that it is "a temple of God." A temple is a place where one worships. We acknowledge that worship is something we do for God and not something God does for us. Worship is not a spectator sport. Worship is not for entertainment. Worship is something we bring to God. Worship involves our confession of sin, the acceptance of God's grace, and the receiving of our commission to go into the world and serve in Christ's name. We have it all twisted around when we think church is supposed to meet our needs. We come to acknowledge our dependence upon God and to serve God.

Baptists have always given each congregation the freedom to determine its own style of worship. The traditions have varied, from the higher church approach of the Charleston tradition (the oldest Baptist tradition in our country), to the Sandy Creek, Ketockton, and Warren styles, and on to the frontier style. Each worked with the other without imposing one tradition as the only Baptist way.

Every local Baptist church is called to be responsible under Christ. We are called to be agents of reconciliation. We seek to minister to those within our fellowship to help them bear their burdens and to train others within our fellowship how to serve Christ more effectively. But we are also charged to reach beyond our doors to the people in the world who do not know Christ. We are an evangelistic and mission-oriented people. Jesus said, "As my Father has sent me, even so send I you" (John 20:21). "Go ye therefore into all the world and make disciples of all nations" (Matt 28:19). We are to go as ambassadors for Christ to bring others to a saving knowledge of Jesus Christ as Lord. We can never be content with the local church as a nice little club and think it is wonderful as an end in itself. We have been commissioned to reach others for Christ. Our purpose is to continue the ministry Christ began.

William Willimon tells about a man in Iowa who wanted to get married. This man had the image of an ideal wife in mind. He had thought about marriage for a long time and dreamed about finding this ideal wife. One day he met a beautiful woman who seemed to fit his ideal. So they got married. But he soon discovered that, though she was beautiful, there were times she was not so beautiful, especially early in the morning. Although she was intelligent, there were great gaps in her knowledge. Marriage was not like his dream. He had to put up with curlers in his wife's hair at night. He had visits from her relatives from Oklahoma, and he had to endure that grotesque lamp she bought. Soon his love for his wife began to wane. He began to dream again about the ideal wife and longed for the perfect marriage partner.[16]

Do you get the picture? So many people move from one local church to another looking for the ideal church. But it doesn't exist in this world, does it? Every church has its warts and blemishes, strengths and weaknesses. Because you and I are a part of the local church, it will always be a not-so-holy church. But that has been the nature of the church down through the ages, hasn't it? The church is composed of the saintly and the salty, the caring and the crude, the loving and the lackadaisical, the holy and the haughty, the faithful and the foolish, the sympathetic and the stern, the hopeful and the hateful. But the church has always had the same kind of people in it. People with faults and weaknesses were in the church from the beginning. When Peter made his confession of faith and Jesus said, "On this rock I will build my church," a weak human being was part of the foundation.

The church is built on this kind of foundation (Eph 2:20). The church was built not on Peter but on the faith and confession of people like Peter and other believers down through the ages who would confess that Jesus Christ is Lord. Sometimes these people were weak, sometimes insecure, and sometimes doubting. But the church has been founded on Peter, James, John, Lydia, Mary, Martha, and thousands of others like them through the ages.

We do our best work for God as we work faithfully through the local congregation, aware that we are not a perfect church. Nevertheless, we seek to let God minister to us and through us in the local church. I am proud of our Baptist heritage and its concept of the autonomy of the local church. But remember, every local church stands under the Lordship of Jesus Christ.

NOTES

[1] Paul Minear, *Images of the Church in the New Testament* (Philadelphia: Westminster Press, 1960).

[2] Dale Moody, *Christ and the Church* (Grand Rapids: William B. Eerdmans, 1963), 62.

[3] Sydnor L. Stealey, *A Baptist Treasury* (New York: Thomas Y. Crowell Co., 1958), 288.

[4] Ibid., 292.

[5] "The Abstract of Principles," article XIV, Southern Baptist Theological Seminary.

[6] Walter B. Shurden, ed., *The Life of Baptists in the Life of the World* (Nashville: Broadman Press, 1985), 19.

[7] James D. Smart, *The Rebirth of Ministry* (Philadelphia: Westminster Press, 1960), 152.

[8] H. Wheeler Robinson, *The Life and Faith of the Baptists* (London: Kingsgate Press, 1946), 73.

[9] George R. Beasley-Murray, *Baptism in the New Testament* (Grand Rapids: William B. Eerdmans, 1962), 304.

[10] Robinson, *Life and Faith*, 77.

[11] J. B. Weatherspoon, *Theron Rankin, Apostle of Advance* (Nashville: Broadman Press, 1958), 117.

[12] W. L. Lumpkin, *Baptist Confessions of Faith* (Philadelphia: Judson Press, 1957), 286-87.

[13] Robinson, *Life and Faith*, 91.

[14] B. R. White, ed., *Association Records of the Particular Baptists of England, Wales and Ireland to 1660—Part 3: The Abingdon Association* (London: Baptist Historical Society, 1974), 126-27.

[15] Lumpkin, *Baptist Confessions of Faith*, 166.

[16] William Willimon, *What's Right with the Church* (San Francisco: Harper & Row, 1985), 1-2.

CHAPTER FIVE

The Priesthood of Believers

Throughout the history of Baptists, the doctrine of the priesthood of believers has resounded like the pealing of church bells as they summon Christians to worship. This doctrine has affected every belief we hold. It undergirds our understanding of salvation by faith, the right of each person to interpret the Scriptures for himself or herself, our church polity and government, our rejection of reeds, and our understanding of the church's ministry and who is a minister in the church.

The Baptist doctrine of the priesthood of believers is rooted in the Scriptures, but the teachings of Luther and Calvin rediscovered this lost concept in the Protestant Reformation in the sixteenth century.

One of our Baptist fathers, John Smyth, in 1608, reflected on this doctrine, which he liked to call "The Priesthood of the Church." He said, "The visible Church by the Apostle is called a kingly priesthood."[1] He cited 1 Peter 2:9 and Revelation 1:6 as biblical foundations for this view.

E. Y. Mullins, one of our noted Baptist theologians and former president of The Southern Baptist Theological Seminary, in writing about the historical significance of Baptists, stated that the great principle that Baptists have attributed to religious thought is "the competency of the soul."[2]

George W. Truett, pastor for forty-seven years of the First Baptist Church in Dallas, Texas, said the priesthood of believers is the "cardinal, bedrock principle from which all our Baptist principles emerge."[3]

Findley Edge, in his book *The Doctrine of the Laity*, calls the priesthood of all believers a "fundamental belief among Baptists."[4]

George W. McDaniel, pastor of First Baptist Church, Richmond, Virginia, in the early part of this century, declared, "According to your belief, all believers are priests and may directly confess their sins, express their praise, and ask for guidance."[5]

W. Barry Garrett states that the priesthood of believers is the "teaching that every Christian has direct access to God through the mediatorship of Christ without the necessity of earthly priests."[6]

Herschel Hobbs, in *You Are Chosen: The Priesthood of All Believers*, states on the first page that "the competency of the soul in religion is the distinctive contribution of Baptists to the Christian world."[7]

What is the meaning of the concept of the priesthood of all believers? My definition is twofold. First, every person has the right and privilege of approaching God directly without any need of another human mediator. Second, every believer then is charged with the priestly responsibility of ministering in the name of Christ and being priest to one another. This concept has led to some distortions or corruptions of the biblical and Reformation view. There can be an extreme position like that of the Quakers who believe the priesthood of all believers does away with the need for clergy. The other extreme sees this doctrine authorizing any private interpretation a person may have, no matter how uninformed or isolated from the body of Christian believers that person may be. Neither of these extremes is correct in the biblical or Reformation teaching of this doctrine. Let us examine the rich, biblical meaning in the concept of the priesthood of all believers.

THE BIBLICAL ROOTS FOR THE PRIESTHOOD OF BELIEVERS

The doctrine of the priesthood of all believers helps clarify our understanding of how we can know God. The roots for the concept of the priesthood of all believers are found in Exodus 19:4-8. In this passage, Moses goes up the mountain in the wilderness of Sinai to meet God. God reminds Moses of what God has done for Israel in delivering them from the Egyptians and establishes a covenant with them. God tells them, "You shall be my own possession among all peoples for all the earth is mine, and you shall be to me a kingdom of priests and a holy nation."

Being chosen by God did not mean Israel would have more privileges than other nations. They were chosen to serve God, not for God to serve them. They were to be a priesthood serving God. The covenant between God and Israel was made with the declaration of God's sovereignty over all the earth. Israel was not chosen to fulfill its selfish ends but to serve God as ministers (priests) to others. The Hebrew word for priest used here (Exod 19:6) is not the common Semitic word for priest used elsewhere in the Bible. It has been suggested that *kohen* can be translated to mean that one can have the right of entree to a king or God.[8] This kingdom of priests, Israel, could approach God directly in worship. The priests were to be holy by being set apart for service to God.

Soon, however, the concept of the nation Israel as a kingdom of priests was distorted, and a highly separate priestly class was established. These priests virtually controlled and guarded the way Israel could worship. Probably nothing indicates the isolation and fragmentation Israel's priestly system created in their worship of God more than the Temple itself.

The layout of the Temple reflected an exclusivistic theology. A series of courtyards walled off various groups of worshipers from each other. As one first approached the Temple, one entered the Court of the Gentiles where foreigners were confined by a wall that clearly stated they could go no further. Next was the Court of Women where women could worship if they were not in some impure state. Behind the next wall was the Court of Israel where men could worship. Behind the next wall was the Court of the Priests. Finally, the inner chamber, or the Holy of Holies, was where the High Priest alone would enter once a year. Each of these spaces was separated by rigid walls so that every person knew his or her proper place before God. "The Temple in Jerusalem was a parable in stone of the Jewish approach to God," William E. Hull writes. "The exclusivisms built into its very structure provided a physical expression in microcosm of the walled-in attitudes of those who gathered there to worship."[9]

DIRECT ACCESS TO GOD

Several of the Gospel writers noted that, when Jesus died after he was crucified on the cross, the veil in the Temple was torn in half (Matt 27:51; Mark 15:38; Luke 23:45). Their testimony was clear: a radical change had taken place. Direct access to God was now possible for all people. The New Testament declaration was that what God has done in Jesus Christ has broken down these dividing walls so that individuals can come directly to God. Paul is clearly dealing with the end of the walls of distinction in these lines: "Gentiles and Jews he has made the two one and his own body of flesh and blood has broken down the enmity which stood like a dividing wall between them. . . . This was his purpose, to reconcile the two in a single body to God through the cross, on which he killed the enmity" (Eph 2:14, 16, NEB). The walls Israel had built to isolate people from God have been broken down through Jesus Christ. Every person can now approach God directly.

We do not need to have some professional priest make intercession for us with God. Jesus Christ himself is our high priest. We can approach him directly. The book of Hebrews speaks boldly of the work of Christ as the high priest:

> Therefore, my friends, since we have confidence to enter the sanctuary by the blood of Jesus, by the new and living way that he opened for us through the curtain (that is, through his flesh), and since we have a great priest over the house of God, let us approach with a true heart in full assurance of faith, with our hearts sprinkled clean from an evil conscience and our bodies washed with pure water. (Heb 10:19-22, NRSV)

The author of Hebrews says that as high priest Jesus Christ is greater than the other priests because he is an eternal priest (Heb 5:6, 10; 6:20; 7:7). His sacrifice was greater because it was a sacrifice made once and for all, while other priests have to come daily and offer sacrifices (Heb 10:11-14).

The death of Jesus Christ broke down the dividing wall that humanity had established through their religious systems. The symbolism is clear: Every person can come directly to God without the need of a human advocate. Each person has soul competency. Every single individual has direct access to God. Neither I nor any other professional clergy nor any person has the right to interfere in your personal relationship with God. You do not have to depend on your pastor to say, "Let me show you the way to God. You must come through me." No priest can say to you, "The only way you can get to God is through me." All human interference is rejected. You can experience God personally through the revelation that was supremely disclosed in the great High Priest, Jesus Christ our Lord. No ecclesiastical or political institution can exclude you from that relationship.

THE NATURE OF THE PRIESTHOOD OF BELIEVERS

Secondly, the doctrine of the priesthood of all believers clarifies the ministry of the church. Several verses in the New Testament set forth clearly who the priests are in the church of Christ: "So come to him, our living stone (to Christ)—the stone rejected by men but choice and precious in the sight of God. Come, and let yourselves be built, as living stones into a spiritual temple; become a holy priesthood to offer spiritual sacrifices acceptable to God through Jesus Christ" (1 Pet 2:4-5, NEB). "But you are a chosen race, a royal priesthood, a dedicated nation, and a people claimed by God for his own, to proclaim the triumphs of him who has called you out of darkness into his marvelous light" (1 Pet 2:9, NEB). "To him who loves us and freed us from our sins with his life's blood, who made of us a royal house, to serve as the priests of his God and Father—to him be glory and dominion for ever and ever! Amen" (Rev 1:6).

These verses tell us something about the nature of the priesthood of believers. Who are these priests and what are their ministries? We acknowledge first of all, as the writer of the book of Revelation notes, that the church is composed of people from every race and nation. "By your blood you ransomed for God saints from every tribe and language and people and nation; you have made them to be a kingdom of priests serving our God" (Rev 5:9). Who is a part of this royal, holy priesthood? This kingdom of priests includes any and every person who is a Christian, who commits his or her life to Christ.

One of the finest artistic representations of the kingdom of priests is in the St. Matthews Baptist Church stained-glass window—the Holy Spirit at work in the world. A central feature of this window is the line of individuals who form a series of patterns of different walks of life across the face of the window. Christ is in the center of this image. On his left, there is a figure who appears to be the apostle Paul writing letters to the early church. Next, one observes a couple, accompanied by a young child, as they are going to work. A chef raises the dish he has prepared. He is followed by two teachers and a laborer working with a jackhammer. This side ends with missionaries sharing the word of Christ with American Indians.

On the right side of Christ, there is a figure of a minister preaching the gospel. Beside him is a young man playing a guitar. Next is a family with a mother and father and three children. Following them is a setting that depicts someone visiting in a nursing home, hospital, or home. This scene also includes a doctor or a friend. They are followed by a farmer. The next figures are either scientists, medical doctors, or pharmacists, and a fireman. On the right end of the window panel, there is an image of a missionary who is sharing the word of Christ with someone in Africa.

What are we to make of this symbolism? I believe the artist is affirming that God's ministry is conducted by people of each race, nationality, sex, and vocation. Every person is a minister—a priest to another. God works in a variety of ways through every single one of us as each of us offers his or her gift to serve in the ministry to which God has called us. People from every walk of life serve in Christ's kingdom of priests.

Believers are called to a holy priesthood (1 Pet 2:5). Holy doesn't mean self-righteous. Holy means being set apart or consecrated to serve God. We are also called to be a royal priesthood (1 Pet 2:9). This royalty does not set us above others in power or position but is a royalty derived from reigning with Christ. Since his reign is a ministry of service, our reign is best seen in terms of service to others in the name of Christ. As priests, we first gather to worship, to acknowledge that our service—ministry—arises out of our experience of togetherness with others in worship. We gather in the community of faith to sense God's presence among us and then we go to serve in his name.

Our calling as priests will lead us to proclamation. We will want to proclaim the good news about Christ to others. This proclamation may be done in a variety of ways. One way may be by a pastor preaching from the pulpit. But the gospel can be proclaimed by a hospital attendant, a secretary, a barber, a baker, a homemaker, a doctor, an attorney, or in a variety of other ways—as many ways as there are vocations or personalities. Any person can proclaim Christ wherever he or she lives and works. There is no limitation and not only one way to share or live the priestly life. Ministry touches every walk of life.

God's Spirit works through all kinds of people, not just professional ministers. The ministry of the Spirit is performed through a variety of ways and with numerous gifts. God's ministry is not confined merely to what happens in a church building. God works through many instruments to accomplish his work. The laity conduct the ministry of the church in the world. God is at work in the bakery, with the firefighter, at school, in the doctor's office, in the secretary's office, with the farmer in the field, in all of life. Believers gather in the church that we might prepare to go back into the world to minister.

The church is not calling ministers to a servanthood of the laity. It is calling the laity to a ministry in the world. You and I gather in church to worship, but then we go back into the world to serve Christ there. We do not serve Christ just when we gather in church on Sunday. We gather to prepare ourselves through worship to go into the world and minister in his name. God works in many ways through people to minister in the world. He employs young, old, teachers, doctors, children, chefs, farmers, bankers, homemakers, and countless thousands of others to touch the lives of people. God has many voices and tongues.

FREE TO INTERPRET THE SCRIPTURES

Thirdly, the doctrine of the priesthood of all believers enables us to understand that every person is competent to interpret the Scriptures for himself or herself without some other priest determining which interpretation is correct. Each believer reads the Scriptures and seeks the guidance of the Holy Spirit to understand the truth of what has been read. Jesus said, "I will ask the Father, and he will give you another Advocate, to be with you forever. . . . But the Advocate, the Holy Spirit, whom the Father will send in my name, will teach you everything, and remind you of all that I have said to you" (John 14:16, 26). As you and I open the Scriptures, we seek to let the Spirit of God speak to us through the written words. No person can assume that he or she has already arrived and has the only interpretation God's Spirit may reveal. God's Spirit is not bound to the past or to past or present interpretations. God's Spirit continues to bring us new truths and insights out of the boundless riches of the Scriptures.

I made a vow as a young minister that I would always be open to God's Spirit. Down whatever avenue of new insight he took me, whatever new opportunities for service lay ahead of me, what future thought he might provoke, no matter where he led me in my thinking, I promised I would be open to God that I might grow in my awareness of God and my faith. One of the sad things about some Christians I know is that they have limited God as though they could capture him and put him in a box. They think they have already learned all they can ever learn of God. For them, there are no surprises, no new opportunities, no fresh insights about God. They hug the shores of familiarity and cling to their security blankets of traditionalism and orthodoxy, fearful that God will come into their minds and give new insights, new thoughts, new wine, or new ways.

An open mind also means we are free and not bound by someone else's religious interpretations or teachings. We sit before an open Bible with an open mind. I am not bound by somebody's teaching from the past. I am not restricted in my interpretation of the Bible by the way some other individual, theologian, denomination, church, state, association, or convention sees it. The doctrine of the priesthood of all believers gives each person the right to interpret the Scriptures.

God's Spirit can never be trapped or limited by our traditions, customary ways, or thoughts. God is always pushing against us to flood our perspective with new opportunities and to find new ways to serve and minister for him. No walls can contain God. No floors are too thick for his Spirit to penetrate. God's Spirit breaks through all forms and traditions to give us newness in life. He touched the disciples and they were transformed. They became people who were excited about sharing his good news with others; they were eager to tell others about what Christ had done. Their enthusiasm was evident and others could sense the new power within them. We continue to await God's Spirit to guide us into deeper truth.

But with freedom comes responsibility. We are free to be informed or to be foolish. You or I can interpret the Scriptures and be completely wrong in our understanding due to our ignorance.

One of the most interesting experiences I had when I was teaching in a seminary was to sit in a typical Sunday school class on Sunday mornings. I saw Baptists at their best and worst. I listened to each person give his or her interpretation of a biblical passage. But, unfortunately, most of the time this discussion was not based on study or research, but on one's opinion. Paul's advice to Timothy was, "Do your best to present yourself to God as one approved by him, a worker who has no need to be ashamed, rightly explaining the word of truth" (2 Tim 2:14).

The best term for rightly dividing or explaining the word was probably drawn from an image of a carpenter cutting a straight line with a saw. Or, since Paul was a tentmaker, he may have used the figure from his own trade in which he had to cut through haircloth in a straight line with scissors. He knew this was a difficult task.

What does this mean? Every Christian wants to be skilled in understanding and teaching the Bible and Christian doctrine. This requires study and research. Many Sunday school teachers devote long hours to study and preparation for their lessons. We all should. If we are going to have an opinion about passages in the Bible, let us be informed. The Bible cannot mean anything I want it to mean. We have to be informed.

John Broadus said his father told him he could prove to him from the Bible that there was no God. He opened his Bible and asked John to read the verse, "There is no God." He then lifted his finger and asked the boy to read what had been covered by his fingers: "The fool hath said in his heart, There is no God." "Now," his father said, "don't you see, you must always attend to the connections."[10]

We have to try to see how any one part of the Bible is connected with other parts of Scripture. As we try to interpret the Bible, we need to share not out of ignorance but by being informed. The desire to be informed was the reason Baptists were at the forefront of ministerial education in our country. That is the reason we have Sunday schools and learning opportunities in our churches. We want our people to be educated and knowledgeable about the Scriptures. Many of our Baptist colleges were originally founded to educate ministers. We did not want our ministers speaking out of ignorance. Whether we speak out of ignorance or we are informed in our biblical beliefs, one of our cardinal principles is that each believer is a priest to interpret the Scriptures under the guidance of God's Spirit.

PRIESTS TO EACH OTHER

Fourthly, the priesthood of all believers means we are also priests to each other. Martin Luther wrote,

> We are also priests forever, which is far more excellent than being kings, for as priests we are worthy to appear before God to pray for others and to teach one another divine things. . . . Thus Christ has made it possible for us, provided we believe in him, to be not only his brethren, co-heirs and fellow-kings, but also his fellow priests.[11]

To be priests to each other means every single person in our church is a minister. Everyone is a minister, not just the paid, professional clergy. All believers are ministers. The word laity means "people of God." Every one of us shares in the ministry of Christ.

The Church of the Savior in Washington, DC, affirms in its membership statement that the Church of Christ is a ship on which "there are no passengers—all are crew members." Each of us is the church in a particular spot. Every Christian is a priest. You need to find your place of ministry.

Every single Christian needs to be engaged in ministry. If we are a member of the church of Christ, a member of this congregation, then we need to find what our ministry is and in what way we can serve and be a part of the vital body of Christ.

We all need a sense of call in some kind of ministry. If I were to ask, "How many of you are ministers?" I wonder how many hands would go up. Usually our church members think of only the professionals as the ministers. The rest of the members of my congregation on a typical Sunday morning are laypeople. But think with me a moment. What is a layperson? I am a layman in many respects. You surely don't want me performing brain surgery or operating on you for a kidney stone! I am a novice in these areas. I remember hearing a lecture on symbolic logic, and, although I was majoring in philosophy of religion in graduate school, this man, a mathematician, spoke so abstractly that I could not begin to follow him. In the area he was addressing, I was a layman. In many areas I am not skilled. I cannot read electrical blueprints or build computers. I am a layperson in those areas.

When it comes to being a part of the church, the New Testament says that we are the laity—the people of God, the called out ones. We all share in ministry. Ministry is not just for the professionals, but every one of us has his or her ministry in the church. Too often, many in the church think that to be a layperson means one can sit back and simply leave ministry to others. This is misunderstanding what the New Testament means by ministry.

I remember watching a basketball game once on television where two coaches got in such an argument in the middle of the court that they were pushing each other back and forth, up and down the floor, while they were arguing with each other. The players gathered around them and began to encourage them. Soon the spectators began to yell and urge them on. The referees stood hopelessly by and could do nothing. But there was something wrong with that in a basketball game. You do not have a basketball game when the two coaches are in the middle of the court arguing. The players need to be out there playing.

Similarly, the work of ministry is not carried on only by the professional people. It is carried on by all of us. Every person has a place in ministry. Each and every one of us needs to find his or her place of ministry in the church of Christ. You have a gift of ministry, and you need to discover what it is.

My wife and I attended a church social for young adults one night and the leader of the group said, "Bill, why don't you trade places with Emily?" I said, "I can't." Oh, I know what he meant. He meant for me simply to exchange seats. Now I could do that, of course, but I cannot take Emily's place. She has her ministry. She has her role. She has her gifts, as I have mine, and each of us seeks to find his or her place in ministry and service.

Our ministries for Christ are limited only by the gifts we offer to him through his church and by our imagination. You are a minister as well as those of us on the professional staff of a church, and each needs to assume his or her particular place of service. There is a great variety of ministries. I hope you will find your ministry and become excited about your opportunity to work and grow.

There is really no hierarchy in ministry. No one is more important in the eyes of God than others. None of us is supposed to be just a consumer. None of us can be merely a spectator and an observer. I like the way Karl Barth wrote about this a number of years ago when he said:

> There can be no talk of higher and lower orders of specific service. There is differentiation of functions, but the preacher cannot really stand any higher than the other elders; nor the bell-ringer any lower than the Professor of Theology. There can be no "clergy" and no "laity," no merely "teaching" and no merely "listening" Church, because there is no member of the Church who is not the whole thing in his own place.[12]

In one of Charles Schulz's cartoons, Snoopy is seen jogging. As he runs, his body begins to talk to him. His feet say, "Man, don't you know what you are doing to me? You are killing me! I can't take this." Soon the calf muscles say, "Well, man, it's kind of tough on us, too." Then the thigh muscles begin to respond, "Well, it's really us that are keeping you going." Soon the arms say, "Well, I give you motion and activity. You have to have me." And the lungs say, "Without our ability to breathe you can't make it."

Finally the heart speaks, "If I stop all of you have had it." As Snoopy finally relaxes on his doghouse later, he comments, "All are necessary. Every one of you guys is important."

Every single one of us has a ministry. You need to find through and in your church your place to minister in the name of Jesus Christ. None of us can be just a passenger on the ship of Christ. All of us are called to be a vital part of the ministry of Christ. Our variety is not a weakness but a strength.

God is the source of all our gifts in the church. But let us affirm that every Christian has a gift. Let us identify and acknowledge the gift of every

Christian. Let us then recognize and affirm those gifts. And then let us apply those gifts to service for Christ to glorify and build up the body of Christ, the church. "Our Baptist churches recognize no priestly class," Rauschenbusch observed. "Our ministers are not essentially different from the laity."[13]

H. Wheeler Robinson has stated forcefully the Baptist rejection of a sharp distinction between the ministries of the laity and clergy:

> In view, therefore, of the New Testament evidence, the Baptist feels amply justified in refusing to make any distinction between "clergy" and "laity" which implies a difference of status and privilege and not simply a function and service. In the wide sense of the New Testament, all Christians are called to minister, according to their "gift"; whatever they are able to do for the service of the community and of the world they are called to do. The ministry of "laymen" in this sense is fully maintained and jealously asserted amongst Baptists; there is nothing which a "minister" in the professional sense is called upon to do—preaching, administration of the ordinances of baptism and the Lord's Supper, the conduct of Church business, the performance of the marriage ceremony, the burial of the dead—which a "layman" as such is debarred from doing.[14]

Every single one of us is called to minister and serve in some capacity for God so that we might glorify him and edify and build up the church. Each of us is a priest to another.

A Servant Ministry

Finally, we are priests who are called into a servant ministry. Religion is personal but it is never private. Our religion is individual, but it is not to be lived out in isolation. We need to be a part of the community of faith and lean upon each other and draw strength and guidance from one another. We acknowledge within our own denomination that there is no hierarchy in the church. The pastor is not elevated above the other members in political power. I, like you, am recognized for my gifts. Every Christian is a servant and missionary for Christ. The priesthood of all believers affirms "the abolition of the laity." Laypeople are set free to serve our Lord as fellow ministers.

Robinson stated this truth like this: "Pastors are, in a word, the servants of the Church. The Church, indeed, is not their master; but they are, nevertheless, its servants."[15] I do not have the authority to say to you that you have no right to pray to God; you have no right to receive God's grace unless I as a clergyperson dispense it to you. In Acts 14:23, where elders were chosen in the churches by conducting a vote, the Greek word literally means "raising their hands." These Christians participated then, as we do as a body of believers today, without one person dictating to them what must be done or what that fellowship must believe.

What is the role of the pastor in the church? A part of the role of the pastor is to help equip and train the people. There is no way that the pastor or staff can do all the ministry in any church. We seek to train, guide, and equip our people. But I am a working foreman. I work alongside you. You also are called to minister. It is a tremendous corruption of the New Testament concept of ministry to think the church is supposed to hire a few people to do all of its ministry.

Apathy, of course, can tremendously affect our concept of the priesthood of all believers. Apathy encourages the laity to want to be spectators and sit in the bleachers. But that is not the New Testament picture of the kingdom of priests. The ministry of the church is not to be the work of the clergy alone. The church is not made up of a Society of Spectators or an Association of Onlookers. The church is not an Uninvolved Critic Society, nor the "You Do It and I'll Sit Back and Complain Club."

The church is called to be involved in the needs of humanity. Every Christian is responsible for service, because he or she is a minister. The call to serve is not just for the clergy; all laypeople are commissioned for ministry. When you were called to salvation, you were called to ministry. If you have been redeemed by Christ, then you have been called to ministry. There is *no* exception. Every single one of us has been called to a ministry of reconciliation and servant ministry for Christ in the world.

What form does the ministry for Christ take? The church under the cross will have a ministry that takes the form of a servant. Just as Jesus was obedient unto death, even death on the cross, so he has called his disciples to a servant ministry. Jesus identified himself with the image of the Suffering Servant in Isaiah. He said, "I came not to be ministered unto, but to minister and to give my life a ransom for many." "If anyone would be first, he/she must be last of all." "The greatest of all is the servant of all" (Mark 10:44). Jesus took a towel and a basin, girded himself, and washed the feet of his disciples. He indicated to them by this act the kind of ministry they should take—a servant ministry. Jesus said, "I have given you an example that you should do unto others as I have done unto you" (John 13:15). His ministry was that of a servant.

The church's ministry is to take the form of a servant in the world. The church is not to be served or to serve us, but to minister in the world through us in Christ's name. Christ has called us to a ministry not to see what we can get out of it for ourselves but what we can do in service for him. A servant of Christ will not be power hungry or status conscious. As a servant, he or she decreases that the Master might increase.

What does all this mean? It means that you and I, as we work in the church, whether we are pastor, minister of education, minister of music, or layperson, all of us are servants if we follow Christ's example. None of us rules over the other. As a pastor, I am not your ruler. You are not mine. We are co-laborers together for Christ. We seek to serve together, not to be honored, but to glorify Christ.

Any conspicuous position in the work of Christ is essentially a ministry or service to God and others. "Do not try to rule over those who have been put in your care, but be examples to the flock," 1 Peter 5:3 reminds us. The pastor is called not to be a ruler but a servant. The pastor's major role is to minister and to equip the rest of the church's ministers for service.

The Church as the Body of Christ

Paul's concept of the church as the body of Christ continues to be a helpful analogy for understanding the nature of the church in ministry. As head of the body, Christ is Lord of the church and is the church's ultimate authority. Whatever authority church members have, they draw from Christ's presence. Although the body is one, there is great diversity within this oneness. Paul's analogy emphasizes everyone's importance within the church. Every Christian, lay or clergy, has spiritual gifts. Just as the human body would be overwhelmed if one part of its body dominated it, so the church would not function properly if one member of its body totally controlled it—even if that person were the pastor.

Every Christian has gifts. These gifts, Paul says, are to be used ungrudgingly in the service of Christ. There is no gift too small or too great to be excluded from the practical service of Christ. Our gifts, which come to us from God, are to be used generously to bring others to know the Christ as

Lord. As stewards of Christ, we serve in his house—the church—and acknowledge that all we have and are we owe to him. As good stewards, we share his grace with others. Everything we have is entrusted to us by God to be used in service for him. We offer our gifts to him so his church can be the agent of reconciliation that he created it to be.

The church is never fully what it should be. We are imperfect. The church is always in process of being rebuilt. The church never completes its building process to be like Christ. God comes again and again to breathe upon the church to make it what it should be.

A number of years ago I read a parable about the church by a man named W. W. Grady, who grew up in central Kentucky. When he was a young boy, his father purchased a sawmill. To his chagrin, the father discovered that one of the main bearings in the saw had burned out. They tried to locate another one but decided the simplest thing would be to make a new bearing. They nailed two smooth boards around the main shaft and the housing. They dug around in their scrap metal and found pieces of babbitt metal. They washed them, cleaned them, and then heated them to remove all the dirt and grit. Then they poured the hot liquid into the mold they had made for the bearing. After it cooled sufficiently, they bored a hole down through the middle of the bearing. When they bored the hole through it, they discovered that it was not a perfect bearing at all. It had little crevices and other flaws. Some thought they should reject this bearing because it was not perfect. But Grady's father said, "No, the flaws and crevices will help lubricate the bearing better." His father turned the steam engine on and the main shaft began to turn. It was not a perfect sawmill. But the huge saw began to sing. The new bearing did its job, and the saw began to cut the wood they needed.

This is a powerful parable about the church. We are brought to Christ as sinners. We come, needing to be washed and cleansed of our sins by the power of his grace. Our sins are burned away by the forgiving grace of his love. Our baptism signifies that we have been cleansed by his love. Then we are put into service for him. We are not perfect instruments. We are flawed and inadequate, but God uses us in his kingdom's work and his ministry goes on.

Our churches are composed of human beings, so we will never have perfect churches. You will never have a perfect pastor or perfect deacons. We are all human beings with flaws and weaknesses. But we offer to God our individual gifts. Each one of us dedicates these gifts to God's service and acknowledges that we serve under the lordship of Christ. We labor in the church not for our glory but for Christ's. I am thankful for the priesthood of all believers for which Baptists have stood since our beginning. Let's not give this cherished belief away and anoint somebody to be our priest when each of us is called to be a minister for Christ.

NOTES

[1] *The Works of John Smyth* (Cambridge: Cambridge University Press, 1915), 274.

[2] E. Y. Mullins, *The Axioms of Religion* (Philadelphia: Judson Press, 1908), 53.

[3] George W. Truett, "The Baptist Message and Mission," in *The Life of Baptists in the Life of the World*, ed. Walter B. Shurden (Nashville: Broadman Press, 1985), 113.

[4] Findley B. Edge, *The Doctrine of the Laity* (Nashville: Convention Press, 1985), 9.

[5] George W. McDaniel, *The People Called Baptists* (Nashville: The Sunday School Board of the Southern Baptist Convention, 1919), 47.

[6] *Encyclopedia of Southern Baptists* 2 (Nashville: Broadman Press, 1958), 1113.

[7] Herschel H. Hobbs, *You Are Chosen: The Priesthood of All Believers* (San Francisco: Harper & Row, 1990), 1.

[8] H. L. Ellison, *Exodus* (Philadelphia: Westminster Press, 1981), 26-27.

[9] William E. Hull, *Beyond the Barriers* (Nashville: Broadman Press, 1981), 26-27.

[10] John A. Broadus, *Sermons and Addresses* (New York: Eaton & Mains, 1886), 190.

[11] Martin Luther, "The Freedom of a Christian," in *Three Treatises* (Philadelphia: Fortress Press, 1960), 290.

[12] Karl Barth, *The Universal Church in God's Design*, cited in *The Realm of Redemption* by J. Robert Nelson (Greenwich: Seabury Press, 1951), 145.

[13] Walter Rauschenbusch, "Why I Am a Baptist," *A Baptist Treasury*, ed. Sydnor L. Stealey (New York: Thomas Y. Crowell Co., 1958), 173.

[14] H. Wheeler Robinson, *The Life and Faith of Baptists* (London: Kingsgate Press, 1946), 104.

[15] Ibid., 102.

CHAPTER SIX

Religious Liberty

Unaware of history, many today do not realize the costly price others had to pay for the religious liberty we have had in the United States for more than 200 years. To earn this freedom, our Baptist ancestors were often fined, harassed, whipped in public, imprisoned, and sometimes even banished from one of the colonies. Both Roman Catholics and Protestants have had a shameful legacy of persecution.

L. L. Gwaltney was a noted Virginia editor. He once told about an experience he heard his grandfather relate. When his grandfather was a small boy, he accompanied his father to the funeral service of an old Colonial Virginia preacher. As he and his father looked at the body of the preacher in the casket, the boy noticed that large scars covered the preacher's hands. Later the boy asked his father about the scars. His father told him that this Baptist minister had been arrested for preaching in violation of the established church. Because he continued to preach from the jail, a high fence was built in front of the jail window so the people who gathered there could not see him. The people continued to gather to hear him preach. When he preached, he would stick his hands through the bars of the jail to gesture.

When he extended his arms through the bars, the guards on duty would cut his hands with sharp knives. He bore those scars to his grave.[1]

Many Baptists today are unfamiliar with our history of scars and the persecution our ancestors had to bear so that you and I might celebrate religious liberty in this country. Glenn Hinson, in a book titled *Religious Liberty: The Christian Roots of Our Fundamental Freedoms*, wrote, "Erosion of religious liberty, as of any liberty, takes place almost imperceptibly. Unless a people are vigilant, they may find themselves without the cherished freedom their faith demands."[2] Religious liberty may slip from our grasp if we are not continually guarding it. Many historians have called religious liberty the greatest contribution of Baptists to the world. Historian Cecil Northcott, speaking of the Baptist witness to religious liberty, states that the Baptist devotion to this idea "makes their place a foremost one in the history of liberty."[3]

In an address delivered from the steps of the Capitol in Washington, DC, on the occasion of the meeting of the Southern Baptist Convention in May 1920, George W. Truett declared, "Indeed the supreme contribution of the new world to the old is a contribution of religious liberty. This is the chiefest contribution that America has thus far made to civilization. And historic justice compels us to say that it was pre-eminently a Baptist contribution."[4] Robert Baker, one of our noted Baptist historians, wrote, "The first appeal for religious liberty in the English language came from Baptists."[5] The late Chief Justice of the United States Supreme Court, Charles Evans Hughes, at the laying of the cornerstone for the National Memorial to Religious Liberty, noted, "This contribution is the glory of the Baptists' heritage, more distinctive than any other characteristic of belief or practice. To this militant leadership all sects and faiths are debtors."[6]

EARLY ENGLISH BAPTIST STRUGGLES FOR RELIGIOUS LIBERTY

While theologians and historians praise the Baptist role in religious liberty, many of us who are Baptists are unaware of our significant role. Unfortunately, some Baptists today are at the forefront of denying religious liberty for others rather than affirming that historic right.

Baptists began their struggles for religious liberty in the seventeenth century. As early as 1611, Englishman George Smyth, who is considered by many to be the father of Baptists, first contended for religious liberty from Amsterdam. After Smyth's death, his followers published a lengthy confession of faith. In it, they declared:

The magistrate is not by virtue of his office to meddle with religion, or matters of conscience, to force or compel men to this or that form of religion, or doctrine: but to leave Christian religion free, to every man's conscience, and to handle only civil transgressions . . . for Christ only is the King, and lawgiver of the church and conscience.[7]

Thomas Helwys, who established the first Baptist church in London, England, with twelve followers, was the first Baptist to write in favor of religious freedom in his book, *A Short Declaration of the Mistery of Iniquity*. His efforts for freedom of religious expression landed him in the London Newgate prison, and he died a mysterious death.

John Bunyon spent twelve years (1660–1672) in prison in London for preaching without ordination or sanction by the established church. When he got out of prison, he became minister of the Baptist church at Bedford. After a few years, he was arrested again. From this imprisonment came his great *Pilgrim's Progress*. Bunyan continued to preach and write from his prison cell.

Mark Busher published his book, *Religion's Peace, A Plea for Liberty of Conscience*, in 1614, in which he presented seventeen arguments against persecution.

John Murton was imprisoned in London in 1612 for his conviction about soul liberty. Since he thought he would die in prison, he wanted to record his views on religious liberty. He had no paper or ink, but he came up with a unique way to record his beliefs. Each day the prisoners were given a bottle of milk with a piece of paper stuffed in the top like a stopper to prevent the spilling of milk. Each day Murton took a sharp object and used some of the milk as ink to write on his piece of paper. One of his friends outside the prison browned the milk on the paper over a fire and transcribed Murton's words into a tract for religious liberty.[8]

The efforts of Baptists in England to press their right and the rights of others for the freedom to worship outside the established English church as their conscience led them finally resulted in the Toleration Act of 1689. This act gave dissenters such as Baptists and others the legal right to practice their faith. The efforts of Baptists were primarily responsible for this victory. H. Wheeler Robinson, a noted English Baptist theologian and historian, observed,

> Throughout the seventeenth century . . . and from their earliest existence, Baptists had demanded that liberty for religious worship which had to be granted, for the whole nation's sake, before the century closed. Baptists were the first in this country (England) to make this demand, and they had taken their full share of the battle, both in the literal and in the figurative sense.[9]

Their efforts were vindicated. Baptists now had a legal right to exist.

EARLY BAPTIST EFFORTS IN AMERICA

From England, we move across the ocean to America where it took another generation before Baptists picked up the cry for religious liberty again. Sometimes Americans mistakenly argue that they want to go back to the religious freedom that existed with the original colonies of our country. But people who say this do not know our history. Religious freedom did not exist when our pilgrim ancestors first landed here. Ten of the thirteen original colonies denied religious liberty and had some form of established church. In some of the colonies, the established church was the Congregational church. In others, it was the Puritan religion. In Virginia, the Anglican church was the established faith. If a person was not a member of the established church and tried to preach views that differed from those of the established church, he or she was often admonished, fined, flogged, and imprisoned.

Roger Williams challenged the established church of the Massachusetts Bay Colony, where the government was a combination of democracy and theocracy. His most famous book was *The Bloody Tenet of Persecution*, published in 1644. When Williams was banished from Massachusetts for his beliefs, he first took refuge among the Indians. He bought land from the Indians and established Providence, Rhode Island, and founded Providence Baptist Church, the first Baptist Church in America, so that there could be religious freedom.

In 1640, John Clarke and several other dissenters announced their views and established the First Baptist Church of Newport, Rhode Island, the second Baptist church in America. When Clarke returned to Lynn, Massachusetts, he was arrested, put on trial, imprisoned, and whipped. Later Clarke went to England and remained there for twelve years, practicing medicine until he received a charter from Charles II that granted religious tolerance for Rhode Island. But it was 120 years later before the American people would really experience religious liberty.

Dr. Henry Dunster, a noted scholar, was appointed president of Harvard in 1640. When he announced in 1655 that he had become a Baptist, he was dismissed and disgraced by the overseers of the college. When the prosperous young Isaac Backus became a minister, he refused to pay the church tax and was put in jail. His widowed mother was also imprisoned for refusing to pay the tax of the established church. She was put in jail for thirteen days and nights. In August 1751, Backus was immersed as a Baptist and continued to serve as a distinguished Baptist pastor. Because of his strong belief that ministers should be educated, he, along with other Baptist leaders, founded Rhode Island College at Providence, which later became Brown University. He authored many pamphlets and delivered many speeches for religious freedom.

On October 15, 1774, Baptists were branded as fanatics in the Continental Congress. John Adams, directing his arguments against Backus and other dissenters, declared, "Gentlemen, if you mean to affect a change in Massachusetts laws, respecting religion, you may as well attempt to change the course of the stars in the heavens." Backus continued to serve as a Baptist pastor until he died in 1806. Eventually, the stars did change their course.

Baptists continued to struggle for religious freedom. They refused to pay the church tax or get a license to preach. Baptists were imprisoned all over our country. In Virginia, Baptists were first imprisoned in Spottsylvania County for preaching without a license on June 4, 1768. John Walker, Lewis Craig, and three others were arrested for "disturbing the peace." Arrests continued in Chesterfield County, Culpepper, and in other places in Virginia. More than forty-two Baptist ministers were imprisoned between 1766 and 1778. Patrick Henry and Thomas Jefferson soon became supporters of the cause of religious freedom.

In 1785, the Virginia House of Burgesses tried to pass a general assessment bill on all taxable property "for the support of teachers of the Christian religion and for places of worship." Baptists organized themselves and led in the defeat of this bill. Thomas Jefferson's Act for Establishing Religious Freedom was introduced in the national legislature in 1779 but was not finally approved until 1786. Jefferson considered this act one of the most important contributions of his life, and one of the three he asked be inscribed on his tombstone. Baptists can take pride in this great document. It reads as follows:

> Be it therefore enacted by the General Assembly, That no man
> shall be compelled to frequent or support any religious worship,
> place or ministry whatever, nor shall be enforced, restrained,
> molested, or burthened in his body or goods, nor shall otherwise
> suffer on account of his religious opinions or belief; but that all
> men shall be free to profess, and by argument to maintain, their
> opinions in matters of religion, and that the same shall in no wise
> diminish, enlarge, or affect their civil capacities.

In 1789, John Leland, a Baptist minister in Virginia, met with James
Madison under an oak tree in Orange County, Virginia, and pledged him
the support of Virginia Baptists in his candidacy as the representative from
Orange County for the Constitutional Ratifying Convention if he would
assure him that after the Constitution was adopted, there would be a Bill of
Rights that guaranteed religious freedom. An agreement was made, Leland
gave Madison his support, and the Constitution was adopted. Madison kept
his word, and the First Amendment was adopted: "Congress shall make no
law respecting an establishment of religion or the free exercise thereof."

Baptists were at the forefront of the battle for the freedom of conscience
and the free practice of religion. The Constitution of the United States
assured Baptists that they had finally achieved their long, hard battle for freedom. For this country's first 220 years, religious freedom did not exist.
Finally, it was realized. Robert Torbet, an eminent Baptist historian, has
observed,

> Democratic America should be eternally grateful to the Baptists
> of Colonial New England and Virginia, for it was, in part at least,
> their struggle for religious liberty which culminated victoriously
> in the omission of any religious test or restrictions when the
> Constitution of the United States was being framed.[10]

THE SOURCE OF BAPTIST VIEWS OF RELIGIOUS LIBERTY

Where did Baptists get these ideas about religious freedom? For one thing,
they read the Bible, which is their basic guide for beliefs and practice. Their
belief in freedom is rooted in the Bible.

The Scriptures vibrate with cries for liberty and freedom. When
man/woman was created in God's image, Baptists believe God gave them the

gifts of individuality and the freedom to become what God had created them to be. Freedom is not merely a matter of choice, but is willed by God's act of creation and redemption. Baptists read the ancient story about Moses standing before Pharaoh with God's message, "Let my people go" (Exod 7:2, 16). They read the words of the prophet Isaiah, "Is not this the fact that I choose: to loose the bonds of injustice, to undo the thongs of the yoke, to let the oppressed go free, and to break every yoke?" (Isa 58:6). "I have broken the bars of your yoke and made you walk erect" (Lev 26:13).

Jesus' first sermon, from the text of Isaiah, proclaimed that he had come to provide liberty for those who were oppressed:

> The Spirit of the Lord is upon me,
> because he has anointed me
> to bring good news to the poor.
> He has sent me to proclaim release to the captives
> and recovery of sight to the blind,
> to let the oppressed go free,
> to proclaim the year of the Lord's favor.
> (Luke 4:18-19)

On another occasion Jesus said, "If you continue in my word, you are truly my disciples; and you will know the truth, and the truth will make you free. . . . If the Son makes you free, you will be free indeed" (John 8:31-32, 36).

Baptists read Paul's letters about freedom in Christ and its radical release from the bondage of religious and political systems and the power of sin. "For freedom Christ has set us free. Stand firm, therefore, and do not submit again to the yoke of slavery" (Gal 5:1). Probably one of the most radical statements about the liberty Christ offers is penned in these lines: "If anyone is in Christ, there is a new creation, everything old has passed away" (2 Cor 5:17).

The passage in Matthew 22:15-22, where Jesus is confronted by the Pharisees and the Herodians about paying taxes, lays down a profound principle about a person's relationship to the state and God. Sometimes politics makes strange bedfellows. The Herodians were committed to the party of Herod, King of Galilee, and therefore paid the tax since they were dependent on Rome in order to stay in power. The Pharisees were rigidly orthodox and would only grudgingly pay a tax to Caesar, which they opposed.

But these two opposing parties joined forces in an effort to throw Jesus into disfavor with the people. They wanted to arrest Jesus, but they knew this might turn the people against them. They approached him with false flattery and asked him what they thought was a "Catch-22" question. They thought they had set a clever trap. If Jesus said, "Pay the tax," that would distance him from the common people who hated this poll tax. If he said, "Do not pay that tax," then he could be charged with treason and trying to lead a rebellion like the Zealots. On what was Jesus' last visit to the temple, the Pharisees and Herodians thought they had backed Jesus into a corner. They turned to Jesus and asked him, "Now what do you think? Should we pay taxes to Caesar or not?"

In a surprising and fascinating answer, Jesus asked them for a coin. It is interesting how quickly they were able to supply the silver denarius. That was evidence of their hypocrisy and their present acknowledgment of Caesar. "Whose image is on the coin?" Jesus asked them. "Caesar's," the religious leaders answered. Jesus then told them, "You give back to Caesar what belongs to Caesar, and you give to God what belongs to God."

This answer by Jesus is a clear declaration that a state does have rightful claims. Christians should be good citizens. In Romans 13, Paul counsels the early Christians that they need to respect the authority of the state. Jews and early Christians were often not good citizens. They were constantly rebelling and trying to overthrow the government. Knowing this view that many held of Christians, Paul may have been trying to help the Christians see the positive side of even a tyrannical government. When Paul was arrested by Pharisees who wanted the Roman government to put him in jail, Paul used the powers of the state by appealing to Caesar.

We are all dependent on the government in many ways. We drive down streets and highways that have been built by local, state, or federal governmental agencies. Street lights, which have been installed by some form of government, illuminate the street as we drive. If we need the fire department or a policeman, or to mail a letter, this is another acknowledgment of our dependency on government. Water, sewage, garbage pickup, and public transportation are benefits of the government. Our taxes are used in endless ways to protect us, to make life better, easier, or more convenient. We are, indeed, debtors to Caesar. The coins in our pockets show that we are already involved with the government. Christians should be good citizens.

George Washington, according to Calvin Blackwell, once said, "Baptist chaplains were the most prominent and useful in the army."[11] Baptists have usually been good citizens and have served in many capacities in their communities.

Sometimes we hear people say that they do not want to have anything to do with government because it is so corrupt. Brooks Hays once told about a woman in the mountains of Arkansas who was being asked by a political pollster about her preferences among the candidates in the upcoming election. The woman looked him straight in the eye and said, "Son, I'm a Christian. I have never voted in all my life, and I never intend to. It might encourage them!" And it might!

Some Baptists refuse to be involved in politics because they think it is dirty. Government from this perspective is seen as an enemy. But other Baptists take a healthier view to work within the political system to bring about change.

Paul goes so far as to say that government is ordained or established by God. In what sense can the state serve God's purpose? Chaos and anarchy are alien to God. God created life out of chaos. Freedom in Christ did not imply license. Paul wanted the Christians to know that they were not free from the civil laws of the state. This would not be freedom but chaos and rebellion æevil.

The state is supposed to promote the civil good of the community. This does not mean Christians are to support any kind of government, even if that state is tyrannical. The book of Revelation describes the government as a beast (Rev 13). When the government assumes the role of God, the Christian citizen is not obligated to obey it. The state cannot claim what belongs to God. Are Christians bound to support the government of an Adolph Hitler? Surely not! We are to render to Caesar his due, but where is the line drawn? The image on the coins of government is sometimes worn smooth. It is sometimes hard to distinguish the limits of government in the realm of religion.

Jesus did not stop with loyalty to the state. He continued, "Render to God the things that belong to God." Here is the real test—our faithfulness to God. The Christian citizen is to give the state what belongs to the government. "Give the state back its money," Jesus said. But our ultimate loyalty is to God. "Seek ye first the kingdom of God and his righteousness," Jesus declared (Matt 6:33). "The earth is the Lord's and the fullness thereof," declares the psalmist (Ps 24:1). We are instructed to give our total allegiance to God. "The LORD our God is one LORD; and you shall love the LORD with all your heart, and with all your soul, and with all your might" (Deut 6:4). Jesus called this the greatest and first commandment (Matt 22:36-40).

The state has limited authority, but God has absolute authority. When the Christian declares "Jesus is Lord," that clearly denotes our ultimate loyalty. We commit ourselves to a God who is greater than the state.

Thomas Helwys, in the first published book on religious liberty, wrote an appeal for freedom. In the quaint spelling and style of the seventeenth century, here is a sample of his work:

> Our lord the King is but an earthly King, and he hath no aucthor-
> ity as a King but in earthly causes, and if the Kings people be
> obedient and true subjects, obeying all humane lawes made by the
> King, our lord the King can require no more: for mens religion to
> God is betwixt God and themselves: the King shall not answere
> for it, neither may the King be iugd betwene God and man. Let
> them be heretikes, Turcks, Jewes or whatsoever, it apperteynes not
> to the earthly power to punish them in the least measure.[12]

Helwys's concept of the separation of church and state was likely based on this declaration by Jesus where Jesus affirmed a clear separation of the powers of the state and religion.

How can people ever say that separation of church and state is not a biblical concept? It is clearly taught in the statement from Jesus in Matthew 22:15-22. God is sovereign over people and states. Man/woman was created in the image of God. Being created in the image of God gives man and woman the freedom to think and act responsibly before their Creator. Liberty implies the freedom to respond voluntarily to God's Spirit.

Every individual has the freedom and responsibility to respond to God without coercion or force. To be authentic, this response has to be free, personal, and voluntary. This is one of the main reasons Baptists oppose infant baptism. An infant cannot respond to God for himself or herself. Someone else has to represent them. Every established church is based on infant baptism. When an infant is born and "baptized" by an established church, he or she is then automatically a part of that state church. But "religion" may never mean anything to this person.

The statement from Jesus about rendering unto Caesar what belongs to him and to God what belongs to God attests that government is subordinate to God. These are not two equal spheres. All things are under the rule of God.

Principles of Religious Liberty

From their interpretation of Scripture and from their own experiences of religious persecution, Baptists have derived basic principles regarding religious liberty. What are some of the great principles of religious liberty that our ancestors struggled so hard to bring into existence?

Opposed to the Establishment of Religion

First, Baptists have opposed any government establishment of religion. No government should make a preference of religion for its people. Yet this is what has happened in a number of countries. Church and state are wed. This was also the case when the original colonies were established in America. The state should not be permitted to use force or any form of coercion to establish religious policy or belief. Our Baptist ancestors stood squarely in the path of the authority of the government in matters of religion. Individuals need to be free to make personal decisions regarding religion. No state should be authorized to try to compel a certain religious persuasion.

In one of Schulz's comic strips, Sally and Linus are going out the front door to school. "I would make a good evangelist," Sally observes. "You know that kid who sits behind me at school?" she continues. "I convinced him that my religion is better than his religion." "How'd you do that?" Linus asks. "I hit him with my lunch box!" Sally replies.[13]

This is the way some churches have tried to spread their religious faith. They have joined themselves with the powers of government and repressed, denied, and condemned any religious viewpoint but their own. To ensure their will, the state has imposed restrictions or laws and prohibitions against any dissenting religious view. They have often not hesitated to use force to compel their theological perspective. "Christ sent his ministers as lambs among wolves," Mark Busher reminded the church, "and not as wolves among lambs."[14]

In autumn 1876, the noted pastor of the First Baptist Church of Richmond, Virginia, and editor of *The Religious Herald*, Jeremiah B. Jeter, wrote a series of articles on "Distinctive Baptist Principles." In the following powerful lines, he argues why force is contrary to genuine religion.

> It is obvious that a church organized on these principles cannot
> be a persecuting body. For what purpose could it persecute?
> Not to force members to join it; for none can be admitted to its

membership without qualifications which no persecution can secure. Not to keep members within it; for it can retain only such as love its members, doctrine, ordinances, and discipline, and force cannot produce these fruits. The conquests of such a church must be made, not by the sword of the executioner, but by "the sword of the Spirit." Other churches may employ carnal weapons, and inflict pains and penalties, to promote their prosperity; but Baptist churches, if they flourish, must succeed by moral suasion and the grace of God.

Hierarchies—churches established by law, and supported by civil, and, if necessary, by military power—have been the greatest curse of Christendom. They are utterly at variance with the spirit and doctrine of Jesus.[15]

Our opposition to state authority in religion also means the government cannot impose any kind of creed, statement of faith, or beliefs upon its people. The government cannot impose taxes upon its people for the establishment of religion or establish a select or exclusive clergy that the nation has to endorse. This belief also denounces any governmental attempt to establish ecclesiastical polity on how churches should be governed.

Religious Toleration Not Enough

Second, religious liberty does not mean religious toleration alone. In England, Baptists and other dissenters finally got toleration in 1689. But in our country, our Constitution and Bill of Rights provide for full religious freedom and not simply the toleration of religion. When the state merely tolerates other religious views, it is clearly making a preference for religion. In his address on the steps of the United States Capitol, Truett made this distinction clear.

Our contention is not for toleration, but for absolute liberty. There is a wide difference between toleration and liberty. Toleration implies that somebody falsely claims the right to tolerate. Toleration is a concession while liberty is a right. Toleration is a matter of expediency, while liberty is a matter of principle. Toleration is a gift from man, while liberty is a gift from God.[16]

No, Baptists have not fought just for religious toleration. We have wanted the right to worship freely, without the government or some other church body condescending to let a group they feel is inferior have the right to worship God as they will. We have demanded religious liberty.

Respect for Every Person

Third, religious liberty acknowledges the importance of and respect for every single individual. We affirm that every person is a child of God by creation and has genuine rights. No one is to be treated as a thing. "The passion of Baptists for liberty is one of their most marked characteristics," Robinson observes, "flowing directly from the spiritual individualism which is their primary emphasis."[17] Every individual has the right to have access to God without somebody else, church or state, seeking to control or dominate that approach to God. If God is sovereign, then the state cannot have absolute power over the lives and thoughts of people. S. Parks Cadman has argued forcefully for the rights of individuals in matters of religion in an article titled "Christ or Caesar."

> If the individual is permanent and the state is transient, it is the height of unwisdom to sacrifice the individual's spiritual interests at the demand of the state. For this reason the history of civil and religious liberty is a history of resistance; of limitation of earthly government, not of its increase. Freedom to become whatever God purposes us to be imposes boundaries on civic authority beyond which sagacious rulers will not trespass.[18]

Freedom of Conscience

Fourth, where there is religious liberty there will be freedom of conscience. Individuals need to have the right to decide whether, when, where, how, or why they will worship. They should be free to choose their own creedal system, nurture their children in their beliefs, expound their beliefs freely, travel freely to share their faith with others, and determine if and how they will support their religious beliefs. Where there is a free conscience, the churches or bodies of worship of these believers should have the freedom to determine their membership, order of worship, creeds or confessions of faith, church polity, selection and education of clergy, ownership of property, formulation of ministries, conduct of evangelistic efforts, and interpretation of beliefs for others. These are only a few of the matters where religious liberty affects the freedom of conscience.

Paul reminded the believers in Rome (Rom 13) that our citizenship is determined by "conscience." "Christian citizenship is determined not by the moral quality of the state, often found wanting," Frank Stagg notes. "It is determined by the moral quality of the Christians."[19] Sometimes our government is wrong in matters of morality, and the Christian has to take a stand against its views. At one time, our government had legalized slavery. But our country was wrong. When our government tried to sanction segregation laws, Baptists came to the forefront of the civil disobedience movement, with Martin Luther King Jr. and others. The laws were wrong. Daniel, Jeremiah, Peter, Paul, and modern Christians have used civil disobedience to protest governmental wrongs.

Freedom for All

Fifth, religious liberty is for all people. As Baptists, we worked to have freedom not just for ourselves or other Christians. Real religious liberty means that a Buddhist, a Muslim, or any person, regardless of his or her religious preference, has the right to worship God as each wills. In this country, people also have freedom from religion. They do not have to worship. They are free to abhor religion, if they like. I may not like that and I may not agree with them. As Baptists, however, we have fought for religious freedom in our country so that any person wherever he or she is can worship God freely or not worship without coercion from any religious body or the state. We sometimes forget how easily that freedom can be abused or lost.

Martin Niemoeller has reminded us how easily this freedom can be lost by apathy or fear. Niemoeller was a Lutheran minister in Germany when Hitler came to power.

> In Germany they came first for the Communists, and I didn't speak up because I wasn't a Communist. Then they came for the Jews, and I didn't speak up because I wasn't a Jew. Then they came for the trade unionists, and I didn't speak up because I wasn't a trade unionist. Then they came for the Catholics, and I didn't speak up because I was a Protestant. Then they came for me, and by that time no one was left to speak up.[20]

Religious liberty requires us to speak up for every person to have his or her right to worship God as each chooses or the right to choose not to worship. We oppose any effort by individuals, organizations, religious bodies or agencies, or official governmental bodies trying to coerce people in matters of religion.

A Free Church in a Free State

Sixth, we believe in a free church and a free state. When I was in Zurich several years ago, I saw the statue of Ulrich Zwingli with a Bible in one hand and a sword in the other. Do you know why he held both? In Switzerland there is a state church. Zwingli led in the union of church and state. Luther formed a state church in Germany. John Knox did the same in Scotland. Henry VIII brought about the state church in England, which still exists today. These churches are controlled by the state and financed by tax money.

As Baptists, we waged a long, costly, painful battle to win religious freedom in our country. We assisted in bringing about the First Amendment to the Constitution of the United States. This amendment reads, "Congress shall make no law respecting an establishment of religion, or prohibiting the free exercise thereof." This means two things: (1) By no establishment, we affirm that the government has no business in matters of religion and will not use state force to propagate religious beliefs, practices, or polities in this country. (2) The government will not interfere with the religious beliefs and practices of its citizens. The Fourteenth Amendment has extended the restraints of the First Amendment to the state as well. This amendment declares:

> No State shall make or enforce any law which shall abridge the privileges or immunities of citizens of the United States; nor shall any State deprive any person of life, liberty, or property, without due process of law; nor deny to any person within its jurisdiction the equal protection of the laws. . . . The Congress shall have power to enforce, by appropriate legislation, the provisions of this article

The *Baptist Faith and Message* 1963 underscores our strong tradition for separation of church and state. It states the matter clearly in these words:

God alone is Lord of the conscience, and He has left it free from the doctrines and commandments of men which are contrary to His Word or not contained in it. Church and state should be separate. The state owes to every church protection and full freedom in the pursuit of its spiritual ends. In providing for such freedom no ecclesiastical group or denomination should be favored by the state more than others. Civil government being ordained of God, it is the duty of Christians to render loyal obedience thereto in all things not contrary to the revealed will of God. The church should not resort to the civil power to carry on its work. The gospel of Christ contemplates spiritual means alone for the pursuit of its ends. The state has no right to impose penalties for religious opinions of any kind. The state has no right to impose taxes for the support of any form of religion. A free church in a free state is the Christian ideal, and this implies the right of free and unhindered access to God on the part of all men, and the right to form and propagate opinions in the sphere of religion without interference by the civil power.[21]

As Baptists, we need to remember that the separation of church and state is necessary to maintain the voluntary nature of religion. Any use of compulsory power by the state would undermine the right of individual decision-making and the freedom of conscience.

From time to time, people attempt to legislate a "prayer amendment" because of the Supreme Court ruling that "required" prayer, Bible reading, or any form of compulsory religious exercises is unconstitutional. Baptists and other groups have reminded believers that voluntary, private prayer has never been denied. Baptists have consistently opposed this prayer amendment effort for two reasons: (1) To subject people to a prayer or religious reading that is contrary to their faith is a violation of religious freedom. (2) Even worse, this practice would give the government the power of formulating prayers, which would be another violation of the separation of church and state.

It has also been interesting to observe that now that Baptists are no longer a minority in this country and have church schools of their own, some Baptists, like Roman Catholics, are trying to get government tax money for the support of their schools. Such aid would clearly violate the First Amendment because the state would be used to support selected religious schools.

We need to be on guard that the church does not try to use the powers of government to support its causes and that the state does not interfere with the practice of religion in the churches. Maintaining this separation is not easy, but it is essential if we are to have religious liberty.

Opposed to Civil Religion

Seventh, we also condemn civil religion. To believe in religious liberty does not mean that we identify religion and country. Civil religion is blending the American way with the Christian religion. Patriotism and religion are linked together in an emotional amalgamation. I am patriotic, and I love my country. But my country and my religion are not the same. Sometimes political and religious leaders have so blended the two that they do not recognize the hypocrisy and denial of genuine religion this kind of wedding produces. Some want to state that our country was founded as a Christian nation. But we have never been and are not now a Christian nation. To assert that only Christians can serve in our government would be a violation of article VI of our Constitution, which states, "No religious test shall ever be required as a qualification to any office or public trust under the United States."

Norman Cavender said he almost fell out of his seat when he read noted Baptist evangelist Tim LaHaye's rationale against the principle of separation of church and state. The powers of government need to be used, he argued, because "revival is not possible without legislative reform."[22] What? We cannot have revival without the support of government? Christianity began in revival that was not state-funded and has continued through the ages, often in spite of the state, not because of its support. Baptists led the battle to be free from such powers. Let's not fall under its binding hold. Bill Moyers concluded his program on *God and Politics* in fall 1984 by observing, "Making biblical doctrines a test of democratic opinion is heresy." [23]

Priesthood of Believers and Local Church Autonomy

Eighth, we affirm the priesthood of believers and the autonomy of the local church. These two beliefs are basic to our belief in religious freedom. As Baptists, we have learned to trust each other because we are priests to each other and priests for one another.

Liberty Requires Continued Vigilance

Finally, let us acknowledge that it is a continuous struggle to maintain religious liberty in our country. It is always possible that it can be lost without vigilance. The well-known Baptist minister W. A. Criswell, followed George W. Truett as pastor of First Baptist Church in Dallas, Texas. On the same television program by Bill Moyers, *God and Politics,* Criswell stated, "I believe this notion of the separation of church and state was the figment of some infidel's imagination."[24] To hear a Baptist make such an observation is so astounding that I hardly know how to respond. We have to keep on contending for religious liberty or it will, indeed, be lost again. George McDaniel reminds us, "As we once took the lead in winning and establishing religious freedom we should now take the lead in clarifying and preserving it."[25]

One of the finest statements I have read on why we as Baptists believe in religious freedom was written by Jeremiah Jeter in the late 1800s.

> We claim for Baptists, however, not merely that they have been the steadfast friends of religious liberty, but that their distinctive principles necessarily compel them to maintain this position. They cannot be consistently Baptists and not advocates of soul liberty. Before they can persecute for conscience's sake, they must renounce, or, at least, ignore their distinctive principles. They may not be free from the spirit of bigotry and intolerance; but it is directly antagonistic to their doctrines.[26]

Whenever Baptists seek to impose their beliefs upon others, seek conformity to their creedal systems, or use any kind of force or coercion to assure their beliefs or practices, they are denying their great heritage as Baptists. Rather than rejecting such a legacy, let us link our lives with the great Baptist pioneers of the past and present like John Smyth, Roger Williams, John Leland, John Broadus, E. Y. Mullins, W. T. Conner, W. O. Carver, Samuel Miller, H. Wheeler Robinson, Walter Rauschenbusch, Harry Emerson Fosdick, Clarence Jordan, Martin Luther King Jr., Lottie Moon, Annie Armstrong, Carlyle Marney, Duke McCall, Brooks Hayes, Billy Graham, Harry Truman, Jimmy Carter, Wayne Oates, Helen Falls, Sarah Frances Anders, and many others.

Religious freedom has always had high priests barking at its heels. Established religion always stays on the back of religious liberty. Religious freedom has had to wage war against the tyranny of those in power, whether they were kings, queens, lords, presidents, or denominational leaders. Religious freedom has constantly fought for its survival against established religion, established government, prejudice, and mass ignorance. If religious liberty is ever lost, we will be losing one of our most precious possessions. It is always worth the battle to maintain it.

A minister named Charles Francis Potter lived in a parsonage located in a well-to-do section of the city where he served as pastor. His salary was not on the same level as that of other residents in the neighborhood, and his children did not have the expensive toys the wealthy children had. They were referred to as the "five-and-ten kids." But the minister's children were creative and formed a club, turning the backyard of the parsonage into a paradise for boys with tents, caves, and shacks. After school the neighborhood kids from all over town would come to play in the backyard, dressed in their ragged clothes. Some of the wealthy kids would gather and watch them play and wish they could participate. One day one of the wealthy children came over and asked the minister's four-year-old son if he could play. The preacher's son ordered the lad to turn around, and he looked at his clothes. "No, go on home. No boy can belong to this club unless he has patches on his pants." [27]

Maybe a part of our problem as Baptists is we do not have enough patches or scars. Having lived in a country where religious liberty has existed for 200 years, we have forgotten what it is like not to have it. Forgetting the long struggle Baptists had to endure to achieve this great victory might cause us to lose it. Let us continue our vigilance.

NOTES

[1] Frank Mead, *The Baptists* (Nashville: Broadman Press, 1954), 31.

[2] E. Glenn Hinson, *Religious Liberty: The Christian Roots of Our Fundamental Freedoms* (Louisville: Glad River, 1991), 22.

[3] Cecil Northcott, *Religious Liberty* (New York: Macmillan Press, 1949), 28.

[4] George W. Truett, "Baptists and Religious Liberty," *The Inspiration of Ideals* (Grand Rapids: Wm. B. Eerdmans, 1950), 86.

[5] Robert A. Baker, *The Baptist March in History* (Nashville: Convention Press, 1958), 128.

[6] Charles Evans Hughes, "Address at the Laying of the Corner Stone of the National Memorial to Religious Liberty," *The Religious Herald* 27 (April 1922): 4.

[7] "A Confession of Faith of Certain English People Living at Amsterdam," in *Baptist Confessions of Faith*, ed. W. L. Lumpkin (Philadelphia: Judson Press, 1959), 140.

[8] Baker, *Baptist March,* 123.

[9] H. Wheeler Robinson, *The Life and Faith of the Baptists* (London: Kingsgate Press, 1946), 132.

[10] Robert B. Torbet, *A History of the Baptists,* rev. ed. (Valley Forge: Judson Press, 1963), 490.

[11] Calvin S. Blackwell, "Baptist Achievements," *The Religious Herald* 11 (April 1907): 5.

[12] Thomas Helwys, *A Short Declaration of the Mistery of Iniquity* (1612), facsimile in the Baptist Historical Society (London 1935), 69.

[13] Robert L. Short, *Short Meditations on the Bible and Peanuts* (Louisville: Westminster/John Knox Press, 1990), 21.

[14] Mark Leonard Busher, *Religion's Peace, A Plea for Liberty of Conscience* (London: Hanserd Knollys Society, 1846), 16.

[15] Jeremiah B. Jeter, *Baptist Principles Reset* (Richmond: Religious Herald Co., 1902), 124.

[16] Truett, "Baptists and Religious Liberty," 87.

[17] Robinson, *Life and Faith of the Baptists,* 123.

[18] S. Parkes Cadman, "Christ and Caesar," *20 Centuries of Great Preaching,* ed. Clyde Fant Jr. and William M. Pinson Jr., vol. 8 (Waco: Word Books, 1971), 121.

[19] Frank Stagg, *Galatians/Romans,* Knox Preaching Guides (Atlanta: John Knox Press, 1980), 114.

[20] Cited in *Politics: A Case for Christian Action,* ed. Robert D. Linder and Richard V. Pierand (Downers Grove IL: InterVarsity Press, 1973), 124.

[21] *The Baptist Faith and Message* (Nashville: The Sunday School Board of the Southern Baptist Convention, 1963), 19.

[22] Norman Cavender, "Freedom for the Church in a Free State," in *Being Baptists Means Freedom,* ed. Alan Neely (Charlotte: Southern Baptist Alliance, 1988), 87.

[23] *God and Politics,* television program produced and hosted by Bill Moyers (Fall 1984).

[24] Ibid.

[25] George W. McDaniel, *The People Called Baptists* (Nashville: The Sunday School Board of the Southern Baptist Convention, 1919), 134.

[26] Jeter, *Baptist Principles Reset,* 123.

[27] Gerald Kennedy, *Who Speaks for God?* (New York: Abingdon Press, 1954), 89-90.

A Selected Bibliography

Alley, Reuben Edward. *A History of Baptists in Virginia.* Richmond: Virginia Baptist General Board, 1975.

Ammerman, Nancy Tatom. *Baptist Battles: Social Change and Religious Conflict in the Southern Baptist Convention.* New Brunswick: Rutgers University Press, 1990.

Armstrong, O. K., and Marjorie M. Armstrong. *The Indomitable Baptists.* Garden City NY: Doubleday & Co., 1962.

Baker, Robert A. *The Baptist March in History.* Nashville: Convention Press, 1958.

Barnhart, Joe Edward. *The Southern Baptist Holy War.* Austin: Texas Monthly Press, Inc., 1986.

Beasley-Murray, George R. *Baptism in the New Testament.* Grand Rapids: William B. Eerdmans Publishing Co., 1962.

Brackney, William H., editor. *Baptist Life and Thought: A Source Book.* Valley Forge PA: Judson Press, 1998.

Brooks, Oscar S. *The Drama of Decision: Baptism in the New Testament.* Peabody MA: Hendrickson Publishers, Inc., 1987.

Childers, James Saxon, editor. *A Way Home: The Baptists Tell Their Story*. New York: Holt, Reinhart, Winston, 1964.

Christian, John T. *A History of the Baptists*. Nashville: Sunday School Board, 1922.

Copeland, E. Luther. *The Southern Baptist Convention and the Judgment of History*. Lanham: University Press of America, 2002.

Cothen, Grady C. *The New SBC: Fundamentalism's Impact on the Southern Baptist Convention*. Macon: Smyth & Helwys, 1995.

_____, *What Happened to the Southern Baptist Convention? A Memoir of the Controversy*. Macon: Smyth & Helwys, 1993.

_____, and James M. Dunn, *Soul Freedom: Baptist Battle Cry*. Macon: Smyth & Helwys, 2000.

Deweese, Charles W. *Baptist Church Covenants*. Nashville: Broadman Press, 1990.

_____, editor. *Defining Baptist Convictions: Guidelines for the Twenty-First Century*. Franklin TN: Providence House Publishers, 1996.

Duncan, Pope. *Our Baptist Story*. Nashville: Convention Press, 1958.

Encyclopedia of Southern Baptists, 4 volumes. Nashville: Broadman Press, 1958–1971.

Frost, J. M., editor. *Baptist Why and Why Not*. Nashville: Sunday School Board, 1900.

George, Timothy, and David S. Dockery, editors. *Baptist Theologians*. Nashville: Broadman Press, 1990.

Goodwin, Everett C., editor. *Baptists in the Balance*. Valley Forge PA: Judson Press, 1997.

Gustad, Edwin S., editor. *Baptist Piety: The Last Will and Testimony of Obadiah Holmes*. New York: Arro Press, 1980.

Hastings, C. Brownlow. *Introducing Southern Baptists: Their Faith and Practice*. New York: Paulist Press, 1981.

Hays, Brooks, and John E. Steely. *The Baptist Way of Life*. Englewood Cliffs NJ: Prentice-Hall, Inc., 1963.

Hill, Samuel S., Jr., and Robert G. Torbet. *Baptists North and South*. Valley Forge: Judson Press, 1964.

Hinson, E. Glenn. *Religious Liberty*. Louisville: Glad River Publications, 1991.

Hiscox, Edward T. *The Hiscox Guide for Baptist Churches*. Valley Forge: Judson Press, 1964.

Hobbs, Herschel H. *You Are Chosen: The Priesthood of All Believers*. San Francisco: Harper & Row, 1990.

Horr, George Edwin. *The Baptist Heritage*. Philadelphia: Judson Press, 1923.

Hudson, Winthrop S., editor. *Baptist Concepts of the Church*. Philadelphia: Judson Press, 1959.

Humphreys, Fisher. *The Way We Were: How Southern Baptist Theology Has Changed and What It Means to Us All*. Macon: Smyth & Helwys, 2002.

———, and Philip Wise. *Fundamentalism*. Macon: Smyth & Helwys, 2004.

James, Robison B., editor. *The Unfettered Word: Southern Baptists Confront the Authority-Inerrancy Question*. Waco TX: Word, 1987.

———, and David S. Dockery, editors. *Beyond the Impasse? Scripture Interpretation, and Theology in Baptist Life*. Nashville: Broadman, 1992.

Jeter, Jeremiah B., *Baptist Principles Reset*. Richmond: Religious Herald Co., 1902.

Leonard, Bill J. *A Sourcebook for Baptist Heritage*. Nashville: Broadman, 1990.

———. *Baptist Ways: A History*. Valley Forge PA: Judson Press, 2003.

———, editor. *Dictionary of Baptists in America*. Downers Grove IL: InterVarsity Press, 1994.

———. *God's Last and Only Hope: The Fragmentation of the Southern Baptist Convention*. Grand Rapids: William B. Eerdmans Publishing Co., 1990.

Lumpkin, William L. *Baptist Confessions of Faith*. Philadelphia: Judson Press, 1959.

———. *Baptist Foundations in the South*. Nashville: Broadman Press, 1961.

McBeth, H. Leon. *The Baptist Heritage: Four Centuries of Baptist Witness*. Nashville: Broadman Press, 1987.

————. *Women in Baptist Life.* Nashville: Broadman Press, 1979.

McDaniel, George W. *The People Called Baptists.* Nashville: The Sunday School Board, 1919.

McKibbens, Thomas R., Jr. *The Forgotten Heritage: A Lineage of Great Baptist Preaching.* Macon GA: Mercer University Press, 1986.

Moody, Dale. *Baptism: Foundation for Christian Unity.* Philadelphia: Westminster Press, 1967.

Morgan, David T. *Southern Baptists Sisters in Search of Status 1845–2000.* Macon GA: Mercer University Press, 2003.

Mullins, E. Y. *The Axioms of Religion.* Philadelphia: Judson Press, 1959.

————. *Baptist Beliefs.* Louisville: Baptist World Publishing Co., 1912.

————, and H. W. Tribble. *The Baptist Faith.* Nashville: The Sunday School Board, 1935.

Neely, Alan, editor. *Being Baptist Means Freedom.* Charlotte: Southern Baptist Alliance, 1988.

Newton, Louie D. *Why I Am a Baptist.* New York: Thomas Nelson and Sons, 1957.

O'Brien, Robert, editor. *Stand with Christ: Why Missionaries Can't Sign the 2000 Baptist Faith and Message.* Macon: Smyth & Helwys, 2002.

Pendleton, J. M. *Distinctive Principles of Baptists.* Philadelphia: American Baptist Publication Society, 1882.

Pleasants, Phyllis Rodgerson. *Freedom for the Journey.* Richmond VA: Center for Baptist Heritage and Studies, 2002.

Porter, J. W. *The World's Debt to the Baptists.* Louisville: Baptist Book Concerns, 1914.

Riley, B. F. *A History of the Baptists in the Southern States East of the Mississippi.* Philadelphia: American Baptist Publication Society, 1898.

Robinson, H. Wheeler. *The Life and Faith of the Baptists.* London: Kingsgate Press, 1946.

Ryland, Garnett. *The Baptists of Virginia 1699–1926.* Richmond: The Virginia Baptist Board of Missions and Education, 1955.

Semple, Robert B. *A History of the Rise and Progress of the Baptists in Virginia.* Richmond: Pitt and Dickinson Publishers, 1894.

Shurden, Walter B. *The Baptist Identity: Four Fragile Freedoms.* Macon GA: Smyth & Helwys Publishing, 1993.

————. *The Doctrine of the Priesthood of Believers.* Nashville: Convention Press, 1987.

————, and Randy Shepley, editors. *Going for the Jugular: A Documentary History of the SBC Holy War.* Macon GA: Mercer University Press, 1996.

————. *The Life of Baptists in the Life of the World.* Nashville: Broadman Press, 1985.

————. *Not a Silent People: Controversies that Have Shaped Southern Baptists.* Macon: Smyth & Helwys Publishing, 1995.

————, editor. *Proclaiming the Baptist Vision: Baptism and the Lord's Supper.* Macon: Smyth & Helwys Publishing, 1999.

————, editor. *Proclaiming the Baptist Vision: The Bible.* Macon: Smyth & Helwys Publishing, 1994.

————, editor. *Proclaiming the Baptist Vision: The Church.* Macon: Smyth & Helwys Publishing, 1996.

————, editor. *Proclaiming the Baptist Vision: The Priesthood of All Believers.* Macon: Smyth & Helwys Publishing, 1993.

————, editor. *Proclaiming the Baptist Vision: Religious Liberty.* Macon: Smyth & Helwys Publishing, 1997.

Spain, Rufus B. *At Ease in Zion: Social History of Southern Baptists, 1865–1900.* Nashville: Vanderbilt University Press, 1967.

Stealey, Sydnor L., editor. *A Baptist Treasury.* New York: Thomas Y. Crowell Co., 1958.

Sullivan, James L. *Baptist Policy as I See It.* Nashville: Broadman Press, 1983.

Torbet, Robert G. *A History of the Baptists* (revised). Valley Forge: Judson Press, 1963.

Tull, James E. *Shapers of Baptist Thought.* Valley Forge: Judson Press, 1972.

Wood, James E., editor. *Baptists and the American Experience.* Valley Forge PA: Judson Press, 1976.

Our Baptist Tradition
Leader's Guide

By William Powell Tuck

CHAPTER 1

PERSONAL RELIGIOUS EXPERIENCE

Baptists are part of the wider Christian community. We share much in common with other Christians and need their support and strength. Baptists, along with other Christian denominations, should seek for the unity of the Church for which our Lord prayed in John 17:20-26. However, we do hold certain distinctive beliefs. One distinctive of Baptists is our belief in a regenerate church membership. What does regenerate church membership mean? A regenerate church is one where every member is a Christian. Each member acknowledges that he or she has been saved by God's grace.

What Does This Emphasis Mean?

- It puts religious experience at the center of our faith.
- Religious experience is essential to church membership.
- The religious experience of each believer has to be a vital personal relationship with God through Christ.
- It means our experience of conversion is by God's grace alone.
- In a regenerate church membership, only believers are baptized by immersion.

Questions for Reflection

(1) What place do Baptists share with other Christians? What beliefs do we hold in common?

(2) Trace the roots you may have as a Baptist through former churches, college or seminary education, or denominational activities.

(3) In the light of large numbers of inactive members in church and nonresident church rolls, can we still affirm our belief in a regenerate church membership?

(4) Define personal religious experience in the light of the variety of conversion experiences.

(5) Do we believe in grace alone when we add other beliefs to the list a person has to believe before that person can become a Christian?

(6) How do we account for such a variety of conversion experiences? Would it not be better or simpler to have only one kind of conversion for all Christians? Why isn't this possible?

(7) Should Baptists modify their practice of baptizing only believers to help their church add more members to the roll?

(8) At what age should a child be baptized? Should preschoolers be baptized?

(9) Do we need to baptize people from other Christian churches who have not been immersed?

(10) Is baptism necessary for salvation? If not, why should a believer be baptized?

Activities

(1) Have one of the class members try to explain to another person (assuming, for the sake of argument, that this individual is not a Christian) what it means to become a believer through personal experience.

(2) Draw on biblical models—like Philip and the strangers on the road from Jerusalem to Gaza (Acts 8:26-40), Andrew bringing his brother Simon Peter to meet Jesus (John 1:40-42), and Paul's conversion on the Damascus Road (Acts 9:1-19)—to depict different types of conversion experiences.

(3) Role-play a baptismal experience and explain to those watching the theological meaning of this ordinance.

(4) Form small groups and ask each group to define the meaning of faith. Ask them to explain the difference between faith as personal and propositional.

(5) List on the board or hand out a sheet with a list of beliefs such as:

    (a) the virgin birth;

    (b) the substitutionary view of the atonement;

    (c) the inerrancy of Scriptures;

    (d) the Trinity.

Ask the group to select which ones a person has to believe to be a Christian. Following the discussion, remind the group that as important as doctrines are, faith is personal—not based on a belief in a long list of doctrines.

CHAPTER 2

A NON-CREDAL PEOPLE

Creeds serve the purpose of trying to explain to others what Christians believe. Their basic purpose is missionary and instructional. Creeds arise out of each age's attempt to explain its beliefs to others. Every generation has to reform, deepen, expand, interpret, and understand its beliefs. Creedal statements cannot be finalized for all the generations to follow. Every Christian needs to have a "theology"—a study about God—that draws on the great doctrines of the church. We gather every week to study our biblical and theological roots so we can grow in our faith. All of our theological statements are limited and inadequate because no one can ever describe or exhaust the image of God, Christ, atonement, the church, or any other doctrine totally or finally. No person, denomination, agency, association, or church has the final interpretation of the Christian faith. As Baptists, we believe the Bible is our ultimate authority and guide in all spiritual matters.

Why Are Baptists Opposed to Creeds?

(1) We believe a personal experience with Jesus Christ is foundational for our faith.
(2) This faith is personal, not propositional.
(3) We believe in the priesthood of believers. Every believer has the right to interpret the Bible for himself or herself.
(4) We believe in the autonomy of the local church. Each Baptist church is free to make its own decisions.
(5) The Bible is our sole authority and guide.

Questions for Reflection

(1) What was the purpose of creeds in the early church? How do we determine the intention behind the creedal statement?
(2) Explain why all theological statements are incomplete. Discuss the human limitation in assuming that one has finalized permanently the view of God or Christ.
(3) What does it mean to say that "all theological statements about God are symbolic"?

(4) Discuss how the Judaizers in the early church attempted to contain the Christian beliefs along the lines of Jewish traditions and beliefs (Acts 15).

(5) List ways Baptists have encountered modern Judaizers today. What has been the result of this rigid approach to our Baptist beliefs?

(6) The preamble statement from the 1962 Baptist Faith and Message states, "Such statements have never been regarded as complete, infallible statements of faith, nor as official creeds carrying mandatory authority." How do you interpret this?

(7) Explain the difference between a Baptist confession of faith and a creed. Is it possible to use the *Baptist Faith and Message* like a creed? Discuss this in light of the way the 2000 version has often been used by inerrantists.

(8) Do all Baptists have to agree on all doctrinal statements? If yes, how do they arrive at this uniformity? If no, are there no basic beliefs that bind us together?

(9) Explain how confessions of faith and creeds can serve as a guide in understanding God and in our understanding of God's ways.

(10) Does a Christian ever "arrive" on his or her spiritual journey?

Activities

(1) Give everyone a copy of the Creed of Nicaea. Ask the group to explain what it means and whether or not they can affirm this statement. Is it necessary to affirm it as it is written?

(2) Write on the board the statement "Jesus is Lord." Discuss what that means. Is it a creed? Is it theChristian creed?

(3) Form groups and have each group compose a list of essential doctrines of the faith. Compare each group's listings. Note the similarities and differences. Discuss whose list is the correct one.

(4) Have several people role-play modern Judaizers. Have them compose a list of creedal statements they think are essential. Try to impose them on the group and insist that, if others do not agree with them, they will have to leave the group and can no longer be a part of the discussion.

(5) Have someone do a Bible study based on Acts 15 and show how it relates to our world today.

CHAPTER 3

THE AUTHORITY OF SCRIPTURE

Although many people own a Bible, few take time to read or study it. Yet it is the church's chief source of authority. As Baptists, we pride ourselves on the fact that we hold to no creed other than the Bible. We also have affirmed our belief that no person or group has the sole interpretation of the Bible either. The Bible alone is our guide for faith and practice. As a record of God's revelation, the Bible does not have to be inerrant or infallible to be our source of authority. God worked through the lives of many people over the centuries to make the divine presence known. The Bible contains history, poetry, prophecy, biography, drama, parables, allegory, sermons, letters, and other kinds of writings to help us understand how God has revealed God's presence and how God has responded to humanity through the ages. The Bible is a religious book and is not a book of science, technology, medicine, or engineering. It is authoritative in matters of faith and religious practice. All Scripture is ultimately judged by Christ. He is the Lord of Scripture and speaks through the Bible to point us to God. The Bible is not an end in itself, but seeks to lead us to worship and serve the God to whom it points us.

Questions for Reflection

(1) What does it mean to say "the Bible is the basis of authority for the church"?

(2) Define and interpret the terms "infallible" and "inerrant" as applied to the Bible and discuss why these modifiers are unnecessary and inappropriate to describe the nature of the Bible.

(3) How did the Christian church get the Bible? In answering this question, discuss the meaning of the Bible as a record of God's revelation and how many writers and centuries were involved in its development.

(4) Are all Scriptures on the same level of authority, meaning, and importance?

(5) Can we interpret all of the Bible literally? What are some difficulties if we attempt to do this?

(6) When Paul writes, "All Scripture is given by inspiration" (2 Tim 3:16), is he talking about books or people? In what sense is the Bible both a human and divine book?

(7) Is the Bible authoritative in the areas of science, medicine, education, engineering, etc.?

(8) Discuss what it means to state that the Bible is authoritative for faith and practice.

(9) Explain Martin Luther's statement: "The Scriptures are the cradle that contains the Christ." If Christ is Lord of the Scriptures, how are we to interpret the Old Testament?

(10) How are we to study the Bible so it will continue to address our needs today?

Activities

(1) Using the *Mercer Dictionary of the Bible* or some other Bible dictionary (which you may get from your church library or your pastor's library) look up "Bible, Authority of" and share with the group the various meanings.

(2) Form small groups and have someone read 2 Kings 2:23-25, and then discuss how we should view that passage in light of the teachings of Jesus who said, "Love your enemies, do good to them who persecute you" (Luke 6:27).

(3) Secure a copy of a Greek New Testament and a Hebrew Old Testament (your pastor may have copies) and ask the group to examine the languages in the text. Ask if anyone can read these languages. Likely not. Explain why translations of the Bible are so important and necessary to reading the Bible.

(4) Have two people select a passage of Scripture such as the creation story in Genesis 1 and 2 and take opposite sides in a debate on whether the passage should be taken literally or not.

(5) Form a circle, or form small groups, and give members an opportunity to share how the Bible has been a meaningful resource in their spiritual development.

CHAPTER 4

THE AUTONOMY AND VITALITY OF THE LOCAL CHURCH

The New Testament is filled with many images of the church both as universal and local in nature. Christ is depicted as the Head of the church. A local congregation is supposed to be composed of people who have committed their lives to Jesus Christ as Lord. After a person has made a confession of faith, he or she is baptized by immersion. Baptism is a sign of the believer's identification with Christ in his death and resurrection. A local Baptist church has self-government, and no person or group can dictate how that church should conduct its worship, business affairs, or ministries. Local Baptist churches are free to cooperate with other Baptist churches in associations, conventions, alliances, or conferences as they determine. This is done on a voluntary basis and all monies contributed to those groups are made by the local church and not by the organizations with which they may align themselves. The style of worship and ministries are determined by the local members as they sense the leadership of God.

Questions for Reflection

(1) What does the New Testament mean when it depicts the church as "the body of Christ"?

(2) Discuss the difference between the local and universal church.

(3) Who should be members of a church? How is this membership determined?

(4) What is the meaning of Paul's statement that Christ is the head of the church? (Eph 1:22)

(5) Why do Baptist churches require believers to be baptized? At what age is a child old enough to be baptized?

(6) Define the phrase "the autonomy of the local church."

(7) Can Baptists speak about the Baptist church?

(8) Should Baptists cooperate with other Baptist churches? What are the benefits or problems with these alliances?

(9) Is there ever a time to disassociate from a convention or body of churches?

(10) Who should determine how a Baptist church conducts worships and selects its ministers and leaders? Can a woman serve as pastor? Who determines that?

Activities

(1) Have someone in the group address the concept of believer's baptism as "an acted parable." Explain the rich symbolism in the act of baptism.

(2) Form small groups and ask each group to make a list of the strengths and weaknesses of the local church. Let them have a discussion in their group and then share their list for discussion with the larger group.

(3) Role-play a church business meeting where the pastor assumes the attitude that he or she is the ruler of the church and pontificates his or her position over the wishes of the rest of the congregation. Discuss how the group feels about that approach.

(4) Ask someone ahead of time to get a list of the various other groups with which your church is affiliated, such as the local association, state convention, and national or international group. Discuss how you feel about being a part of these various groups and, if you do, why you support them financially.

(5) Have the group become a worship committee and plan your Sunday morning worship service. Include whatever you want to have in the service and discuss why.

CHAPTER 5

THE PRIESTHOOD OF BELIEVERS

The priesthood of believers is a fundamental belief among Baptists. Baptists affirm that all believers are priests before God and may directly confess their sins, express their praise, affirm their faith, and ask for guidance. All human interference is rejected. No person or ecclesiastical or political institution is necessary for a person to relate to God. Every believer brings his or her gifts directly to God and functions as a priest to one another. Every gift is important in the ministry of the church. As priests, we gather to worship but scatter to go into the world to serve in Christ's name. Every believer is competent and free to interpret the Scriptures for himself or herself without some other priest giving the only interpretation. With this freedom comes the responsibility for every Christian to be informed and to continue to grow in the faith and knowledge of Christ. As priests with and to one another, we are co-laborers together for Christ. We strive not to be honored but to glorify Christ.

Questions for Reflection

(1) What is the basic meaning of the belief "the priesthood of believers"?

(2) What are the biblical roots for this belief?

(3) How does the doctrine of the priesthood of believers impact the ministry of the church?

(4) What are the benefits and dangers of the principle that each believer is a priest to interpret the Scriptures under the guidance of God's Spirit?

(5) Discuss what it means to affirm that every believer has a gift to be used in ministry.

(6) What is the role of the professional staff of a church and the laity in the order and importance of ministry?

(7) If every Christian is a priest, where does each one minister?

(8) What role does spiritual education play in enabling every believer to have an informed interpretation of the Bible and theology?

(9) Can a person believe anything he or she wants in the name of the priesthood of the believer and still be a Baptist?

(10) What is the biblical understanding of servant ministry?

Activities

(1) List various definitions of the doctrine of the priesthood of the believers. Discuss their meanings.

(2) Form small groups and discuss how people can be priests to each other.

(3) Have someone sketch the Holy Spirit Window and then note the variety of ways one can use his or her gifts in ministry for Christ.

(4) Form pairs and let each person share with the other what he or she sees as his or her own gifts and then speak about the spiritual gifts he or she sees in the other person.

(5) Read the parable about the sawmill and discuss its implications for the church and its ministry today.

CHAPTER 6

RELIGIOUS LIBERTY

Many historians assert that religious liberty may be the greatest contribution Baptists have given to the world. Our early Baptists in England struggled for religious freedom in the seventeenth century. Roger Williams, John Clarke, Henry Dunster, John Leland, and others fought for religious liberty in our country during the seventeenth and eighteenth centuries. Baptists were at the forefront in the struggle during our country's first 220 years for the freedom of conscience and the free practice of religion. That struggle finally led to Jefferson's Act for Establishing Religious Freedom (1786) and the First Amendment to the Constitution of the United States. Baptists have continued to wage the battle for the freedom of conscience, freedom for all people, a free church in a free state, and the opposition to civil religion. Today, as much as ever, Baptists have to engage in a continuous struggle to maintain religious liberty in our country. It is an ongoing battle and requires constant vigilance.

Questions for Reflection

(1) What does religious liberty mean?

(2) Discuss the role that George Smyth, Thomas Helwys, John Bunyon, John Clarke, Roger Williams, Henry Dunster, and others had in the struggle for religious liberty.

(3) Discuss the meaning of the Act for Establishing Religious Freedom by Jefferson.

(4) What are the biblical sources for religious liberty?

(5) What are some principles of religious liberty?

(6) What does the concept of the separation of church and state mean?

(7) Do England, Scotland, and Switzerland have a free church in a free state? Note how these churches differ from the churches in the United States.

(8) Do you think that there should be a "prayer amendment" to our constitution? Explain your answer.

(9) Can the church assume we will always have religious liberty in our country? If not, why?

(10) Should any religious group try to force its views upon others by use of local, state, or national government?

Activities

(1) Select individuals to present a brief historical sketch of the early Baptist's struggle for religious liberty. Draw from the text or Baptist histories from your church library.

(2) Have someone make a brief presentation about the biblical resources for religious liberty.

(3) Form small groups and assign each group one of the principles of religious liberty for discussion. Share with the larger group later.